God is in the Kitchen and Other Everyday Miracles

God is in the Kitchen and Other Everyday Miracles

A Daughter's Gift and a Daddy's Love

Dr. John R. Seita

Writer's Showcase
presented by *Writer's Digest*
San Jose New York Lincoln Shanghai

God is in the Kitchen and Other Everyday Miracles
A Daughter's Gift and a Daddy's Love

Writer's Showcase
presented by *Writer's Digest*
an imprint of iUniverse.com, Inc.

For information address:
iUniverse.com, Inc.
620 North 48th Street, Suite 201
Lincoln, NE 68504-3467
www.iuniverse.com

ISBN: 0-595-12325-2

Printed in the United States of America

DEDICATION

To Lori Perkins Seita. Your love is strong, persistent, and epic; without you, there would be no me. No thanks will ever be enough, but thank you, anyway.

To Anorah Elisabeth Seita. Your love is transformative, your wonder and imagination is boundless, and I have been forever touched. Thank you for your gifts.

CONTENTS

ACKNOWLEDGEMENTS

Janna Brendtro was fabulous and detailed with her editorial corrections; thank you for your focus and expertise. Likewise, Sally Veeder, Vicki Vink, Chris Aube, Nanette Keiser, Shug Brandell, Dianne Price and Lori Perkins Seita all offered useful suggestions in editing this book. Dr. Waln Brown, President of the William Gladden Foundation, provided important editorial suggestions. Plus, he is a fellow traveler along the road of overcoming substantial youthful obstacles and is a survivor and a friend.

Dr. Tyrone Baines and Dr. Joyce Brown are two people of substance, energy, intelligence and integrity. You gave me the opportunity of a lifetime; we certainly are related and I will ever thank you. My friend Connie Binsfeld, former Lt. Governor of Michigan, gave me a chance to shine in front of child welfare experts everywhere.

Continuing appreciation is warranted for a host of caring staff from the Starr Commonwealth Schools, both men and women too numerous to mention. Thank you, you are heroic. Mike Amundsen, my longtime friend from Starr and fellow author, is to be lauded for his normalcy.

FOREWORD

Larry K. Brendtro, Ph.D.
President, Reclaiming Youth International

What follows are the most penetrating accounts about parenting you are ever likely to read. This book is even more remarkable since its author writes from the background of growing up as a profoundly unparented child. Years of deprivation might have rendered John Seita delinquent or emotionally damaged. Instead, he found the spiritual strength to emerge as a resilient survivor.

In his first book, Dr. John Seita recounted his own personal journey from outcast child to child development expert. Now, in this small volume, John shares his uncommon wisdom on parenting as we join him on the intimate journey of fathering his daughter Anorah. This father looks beneath the surface skirmishes of child-rearing to discover the life-altering lessons that parents can learn with their children. His approach to parenting is rooted in a profound spiritual respect of the child, a bold contrast to his own demeaning upbringing.

John Seita never knew his biological father. His teen mother married an abusive man who John believed to be his real dad. That marriage was ended when the adoptive father was incarcerated for spouse abuse. Then, at age eight, the juvenile court permanently removed John from his mother because of her alcoholism and prostitution.

Whatever her weaknesses, John's mother had taught her boy to ask God for help in times of trouble. Warehoused in an abusive institution, young John prayed daily that his Father in Heaven would rescue him. One day his adoptive father reappeared, but only to reveal to John his real paternity, and to announce that henceforth John would have to look elsewhere to find a father.

Now a deeply wounded psychological orphan, John would rebuff all attempts by adults to nurture or discipline him. For the next several years, he ran away from or was kicked out of a long string of placements in foster care and children's institutions. I first met John when a Cleveland juvenile judge sent him to Starr Commonwealth, a Michigan program for troubled boys that I directed in those years. Starr Commonwealth was John's last chance, and it became his first connection. John recalls how "tenaciously caring adults" restored him to the human bond. John Seita would live at Starr Commonwealth from age 12 until he entered college. While he would face many other challenges, in time, John would find success in education, vocation, and in relationships with a loving wife and daughter.

This book makes an important contribution to increasing understanding about the challenges of fathering. In our culture, many young girls grow up playing mother. But, males typically see child rearing as a female role and give little thought to fatherhood until this responsibility is thrust upon them. We are only beginning to realize the enduring influence that fathers have on their children of either gender.

My own son, Daniel, shared with me a moving story of father power drawn from the writings of James Herriott. A young veterinarian is called out to deliver sheep in the icy rain. Hours later, in the middle of the night, he returns shivering to his bed. Now warmed by his wife, he recalls the moment he first knew what a wonderful partner she would be. It was the way she looked into the eyes of her own father – with complete trust, admiration and loyalty. That father bond had laid down the model for relationships with her children and spouse.

Increasingly, I encounter dads who are hungering for ideas about how they can successfully parent their children. On a long cab ride from the suburbs into the city of Chicago, my Russian-born driver showed unusual interest in my work with youth, peppering me with continual questions. Finally, with great seriousness he announced:

> In Russia, I was a coach, and I am very good at working with young boys. However, my wife and I now have our own child, and she is a beautiful little girl. I am terrified because I don't know anything about raising girls. In only ten minutes, we will arrive at your destination. Would you please use that time to explain what I need to know to be a good father to my girl?

I told the young Russian father that each day of his life would bring new opportunities to guide his little girl towards becoming a fine young woman. Of course, many times he would be unsure about just what to say to her. But he always could treat her with the respect that he would want her to receive when one day she would leave her home to seek a partner for her life's journey.

I wish I knew the address of that Chicago cab driver so I could send him a copy of John Seita's book. It charts the pathway of parenting built on respect for the child as a sacred being. As he recounts the small miracles of fathering Anorah, John describes the miracles that all parents and children can give to one another. When I recall that abandoned, angry, defiant boy I first met three decades ago, it is another miracle that he is now a professional colleague in reclaiming youth.

In *A Farewell to Arms*, Ernest Hemingway wrote, "the world breaks everyone and afterward many are strong at the broken places." So it is with John Seita, whose own sacred childhood was broken by rejection. Who could be prepared better to write about fatherhood? One who spent his early life longing for a father. One who survived that experience to become strong at the broken places.

PREFACE

I wrote *God is in the Kitchen* out of a sense of joy. I am more than a bit surprised to find myself in the position to even be a father. My childhood was punctuated with living in far too many foster homes, children's institutions and detention facilities to count; I recall at least 20 in all, but there may have been more. I also lived briefly on the streets as a young adult. The studies tell us that many children who grow up in the foster care system in America end up troubled and struggling as adults. In fact, almost half of the young people who age out of foster care end up homeless within a year. Even more disturbing is the finding that almost one out of every five prisoners in America is a former foster child. Certainly the odds of shedding the shackles of such a painful childhood experience are improbable.

However in spite of those obstacles, I find myself with a loving wife and a wonderful child; I am living the American Dream. I cannot help but appreciate the wonder and the miracle of being a parent and of being given the privilege of having such a delightful daughter.

I have seen the dark side of life, and now I am seeing the brilliance of life. How could I not share this brilliance? A failure to share this joy would be like spitting in the face of God. I want to share my joy with everyday people, and to share the belief that all of us can overcome great obstacles, and that indeed with love from others, opportunities, setting goals and having dreams, not much is beyond our grasp. Ralph Waldo Emerson once said:

"We are very near to greatness; one step and we are safe; can we not take the leap?"

God is in the Kitchen is not intended to be an autobiographical glimpse into my world, and it is not intended to provide the reader with the full dimensional range of either me or my family. Please read **In Whose Best Interest,** my earlier book for those kinds of details. I simply intend to use our family and our experiences as a vehicle to communicate the wonder of the everyday miracles surrounding all of us.

The intent of **God is in the Kitchen,** is to illustrate three points: 1) Miracles swirl around us daily and they are there for the taking; we need only to listen, 2) Our children have much to teach us, while we as loving parents and adults positively guide and support their healthy development; and 3) No matter how difficult our early life may have been, how painful our past, we can transform ourselves to seize the greatness and divinity inside of all of us that is waiting to blossom. Surely, if we watch, listen, and observe, our children will show us the freshness of seeing the world anew every day.

INTRODUCTION

The visible world is a daily miracle for those who have eyes and ears.

-Edith Wharton

You are about to read some everyday miracles. These miracles found me through my daughter Anorah, my wife Lori, and my own observations. These unexpected gifts have given me a window to the larger spiritual truths of the everyday miracles that surround us and guide us and seem almost invisible. Yet even in the midst of these miracles, many of us march on, not listening, seeing or heeding what is so abundant in our lives. We scramble to seek purpose, meaning, and ponder the apparent random nature of things. We wonder where we are headed.

America has a divorce rate of over 50 percent. Suicide and suicide attempts are always a tragedy and still too frequent. Drug abuse, domestic violence, child abuse and neglect still bedevil our society, and the fact that so many of our youth are disconnected is disturbing. Our young people find themselves pregnant, dropping out of school, underachieving, victimizing others and joining gangs. Many adults are lost, too.

Yet there are ways to look at our world through new eyes, perhaps through the eyes of a child, and to even deal ourselves a new hand in the game of life. By looking through a child's

eyes we can recast our reality and examine the wonder that sur-
rounds us in a fresh way. My five-year-old daughter, Anorah,
who has been my primary inspiration for this book, has given
me the gift of looking through her eyes as I examine and
explore my world and search for that meaning.

Through my search, my open eyes, and by God's grace I discovered everyday miracles such as *God is in the Kitchen, Mr.
Potty Pants, Guardian Angels, Average Ice Water, The Detour* and
a host of other insights gleaned from daily experiences. Most of
these hopeful story lessons I have learned directly from Anorah.
Nearly daily, if I listen and watch, I continue to learn the many
everyday miracles that she unknowingly shares with me. I hope
that you will find delight and meaning in them as I have.

I must confess, though, that my joy and delight at being a
father and learning these spiritual lessons are wholly unexpected
but just as wholly welcomed. I did not consider fatherhood to
be in the cards for me. Artist Norman Rockwell's view of
America, with its idyllic and well-scrubbed cherub faced children playing happily under the watchful gaze of protective parents and neighbors did not look anything like my childhood.
My earliest memories are not happy ones as I noted in my earlier
book, ***In Whose Best Interest?***

> *As a five-year-old, I watched my adoptive father
> relentlessly beat my mother. During a short
> argument at dinner, he exploded at my mother and
> nearly jumped over the kitchen table, the one that
> we'd gotten at a garage sale, pulled her forcefully
> from her chair, grabbed her by the hair and threw
> her against the wall. He banged her head repeatedly*

against the kitchen wall. The thump, thump, thump of her head bouncing off of the wall sometimes even now makes an impression in my mind; I can still hear it. After only a few seconds of this beating, I saw blood gushing from her skull and then splatter on the wall. She screamed that she was "seeing stars." I remember her pleading that he "may as well go ahead and kill her." Then he abruptly stopped beating her, loaded us into an old blue Pontiac, and drove my battered mother to the hospital emergency room. Shortly thereafter, they were divorced and my life soon took a turn for the worse, if you can imagine that.

Having survived my parents' brutal and short-lived marriage, I was next subjected to the world of abject poverty, alcoholism, deprivation, decay and madness that was the inner city of Cleveland, Ohio. My mother had given birth to me when she was only a teenager, and she had few parenting or job skills. I guess that she was not prepared to care for my younger half-brother Jimmy, my half-sister Maria, or me as I shared in *In Whose Best Interest?*

When the women's bureau investigated the home there was no food; there were broken beer bottles strewn on the floor and the place was in a state of utter dishevelment. The mother had been leaving the children unsupervised most of the time. The children were all very undernourished.

The Ohio child welfare system, in my judgment, rightfully took Jimmy and me away from my mom when I was eight years old. Jimmy and I were sentenced by the court system to live in a gray, smelly, ramshackle, and decrepit building in inner city Cleveland that housed a children's institution known as the Receiving Home.

The night that they took me away from my mom's poorly maintained and filthy inner city apartment, I was angry, terrified, confused, lonely, and not sure what was going to happen next. My sad and soulful wails of abandonment that first night after being ripped away from my mother must have reached even the furthest settlements of the universe. A lonely vigil found me kneeling and praying beside the rusty, metal-framed bed with the urine-stained mattress to ease my pain.

My mother, in spite of her irresponsible and carousing life style, had taught me how to say the Rosary and to pray to God. I turned to prayer then and hundreds of Hail Mary's poured from my quivering lips in the fervent hope that this was just a bad dream and not a premature trip into hell. I prayed that at the very least the Virgin Mother would rescue me. My prayers became my mantra. I prayed myself to sleep that night and found a short-lived peace that too soon returned to turmoil and despair.

Following that first placement in the Receiving Home, I lived like the Charles Dickens character, Oliver Twist, with life in sometimes-abusive foster homes, soul-less group homes, impersonal institutions and in various orphanages and detention centers. Each placement was worse than the previous one until I was moved into a boys home called Starr Commonwealth. Each movement took away from me a little more of my soul, a little more of my hope, and a little more of my trust. This shuffle between 20 or more different homes in only a few years caused me to distrust adults, and people in general. I frequently ran away from those places, stole food to survive, and was, for the most part, an emotional wreck for most of my youth. My early adulthood was not that much better.

After I left institutional care as a teenager, I was alone with no family and no support, so to give my life some structure I quickly went to college. I soon dropped out, became jobless, homeless, financially bankrupt, married and divorced, briefly arrested and jailed, all within a few years. Sometimes I was suicidal. I never did learn what happened to Maria and have not seen either her or Jimmy since the authorities broke our family up those many years ago. No, I would not prescribe my life at that point to anyone.

Yet, today as a father and a husband, the only bounds that I have are self-imposed. I am joyful, happy, and life is a daily gift. But in spite of all of my blessings, my faith is tested sometimes, and maybe yours is, too. Still, as a father learning from his daughter, I know that there is a God, that He has a divine plan, and that everything, at each and every moment, is unfolding and proceeding as it should.

In the book of Matthew in the New Testament of the Christian Bible, we are told that nothing is apart from God, from the hair on our head to the falling of a sparrow.

> *Are not two sparrows sold for a penny? Yet not one of them will fall to the ground apart from the will of your Father. And even the very hairs of your head are all numbered.*
> (Matthew 10:29-30)

Furthermore, as Richard Bach suggests in his book *One*, *"Nothing is random and events, from the falling of a leaf, to the creation of a galaxy is part of a master plan."* A plan that many of us doubt and seems to be beyond our normal five senses. I think, though, that I've learned to use my senses in a different way, in a way that is almost invisible and seemingly inexplicable but is available to us all.

In her innocence, Anorah has taught me that the answers to life's essential questions may be within our reach, right there in front of our faces. We simply need only to take the time to look and to listen with an open mind, and an expectant soul. When we do so, everyday miracles will roll in ecstasy at our service. Perhaps, after all, life has an order and God in His infinite wisdom is already preparing a life course that escapes our immediate grasp.

This book describes a series of observations that I have made while sharing my life and love with my daughter Anorah and my wife Lori. These miracles, as I call them, sometimes seem to reveal the mystery of God's work. Other miracles may be more practical in that they shed light on how we view ourselves, how we view others, and how we view the world in general. Yet, I am convinced that all of the stories have spiritual underpinnings and serve as the foundation for me to better understand my role and purpose in life as a father, as a husband and as your relative during our visit on Earth. Maybe you too will experience a similar "aha" understanding.

In these observations Lori appears to be saintly and she often is, but not always. Likewise, Anorah appears wise beyond her years; she is wise like a child, a wisdom that I have tried to find again. That these truths are self-evident is manifest by who we are. Inside of us we have God and greatness. We must reclaim our own greatness, put there by the creator, where He resides.

We've all been told that God created us in His image. I've heard that for years, but it wasn't until recently that I understood the power of that message: if God created all of us, and if we all spring from the God-source, then we all have greatness and God inside of us. Sharing these characteristics suggests that none of us is better than anyone else, nor is anyone else better than we are. Therefore, we have divinity inside of us and are born to manifest that divinity. I have found that this epiphany is liberating. Rarely do I doubt my place, my abilities to achieve, and my capacity to contribute to a better family, a better community and a better world.

Most importantly, I think, all men and women are now my brothers and sisters and mothers and fathers and daughters and sons. None are greater, and just as importantly, none are less. We simply are. This knowledge allows us, if we believe it, to walk with majesty among the powerful and elite and with support, understanding and compassion among the poor and downtrodden.

Mark Twain framed this idea well:

Emperors, kings, artisans, peasants, big people, little people—at the bottom we are all alike and all the same; all just alike on the inside, and when our clothes are off, nobody can tell which of us is which.

That consciousness then evolved into the following conversation that Anorah and I have nearly daily. "Anorah, who lives inside of you?" "God," she states confidently.

"And what else?" I ask.

"Greatness," she replies with conviction.

"And what are you?" I ask.

"I'm strong, smart, bold and brave," she answers with vigor.

So, as you read, reflect upon your own greatness, put there by God, and how everyday events are begging for us to learn their lessons. Eminent spiritual scholar, philosopher and teacher Deepak Chopra forwards the idea that *"Sometimes He (God) uses a miracle, sometimes he just makes sure that you don't miss the plane to New York. The fact that anything can happen is the beauty and surprise of the spiritual life."* Chopra also invites us to *"see the miracles around you and that will make it easier for greater miracles to grow."*

Famed spiritual novelist and retired Roman Catholic Priest Joseph Girzone notes, *"He doesn't need melodrama to announce His presence. He works in silence and in hidden ways. His Presence is hardly felt."*

Miracles then should be not seen as rare events of great drama, mystery, and immediate and fantastic transformation. Rather, they are the daily events of life that shape us, save us, and if we understand them, and embrace them, transform us. So while we are out waiting, dreaming, and praying for a miracle of some sort, they are happening daily all around us.

The miracles in this book are not shared in chronological order. They are presented in how they appeared to me in my dreams, in my daydreams, and in my visions. Sometimes I was awake and sometimes not. They beckoned to me while in the shower, while falling asleep, and other times while driving my car or walking the dog. The lessons shared here are really not from me; they are from God, who lives within me and within all of you. These are simple experiences and within the simple, within the everyday, and within the commonplace and the ordinary, may be the divine staring us right in the eye.

Out of parental neglect and abuse, never having met my father, countless movements into all of those "homes" and knowing that *God Is In The Kitchen*, I believe that I have become strong at the broken places. And like Maya Angelou, I would not trade my journey for anything. It is my hope that by sharing these everyday miracles, perhaps you may see in your own lives evidence of everyday miracles and you, too, will become strong at the broken places and would not trade your journey for anything.

God Is In The Kitchen

In a world filled with causes for worry and anxiety...we need the peace of God standing guard over our hearts and minds.

—Jerry W. McCant

"Whaaa! Whaaa! Whaaa!"

"Honey, Anorah is crying," my wife Lori murmured while nudging me gently in the ribs while we slept cuddled in the bed, under a mound of blankets on a bone chilling Michigan winter night.

"Huh?" I replied sleepily, knowing full well what was happening and noticing that the digital clock on the bed stand read 1:57 A.M.

"Anorah is crying, John, and it's your turn to check on her."

"Okay already," I mumbled, realizing that it was indeed my turn and that Lori must rise early to teach in the morning while I got to stay home and be "Mr. Mom."

"Whaaa! Whaaa! Whaaa!" thundered Anorah's ceaseless wails.

"John!" Lori nudged me again after I snuggled for just a few more seconds.

"Okay, I'm up! I think I'll go in the kitchen and get her a bottle. That's usually what she wants."

Pulling the covers off, I was immediately engulfed in cold air and involuntarily shivered. The thermostat was set for 60 degrees on that cold February night. We were frugal with our money. We only had one consistent income, that being Lori's, since I was writing and consulting and we had to pinch pennies because my income, while adequate, was intermittent and unpredictable.

Anorah continued to wail, her pitch picking up in volume, intensity, and frequency. I hoped this wasn't disturbing Lori too much; after all 6 a.m., was only four short hours away and work for Lori seemed much too close.

The house was dark and my eyes did not adjust quickly to the dark, at least as quickly as they needed to in what seemed like a near crisis. "Ouch!" I cried out in pain as I stubbed the big toe of my left foot on the doorframe. I must remember to buy a night light for the hall, I told myself as I felt my way along in the darkness. The cream colored carpeting below my feet was warmer than the air and for that little warmth I was grateful.

"It's okay, Anorah, Daddy will be right there honey. Shhhh, it's okay." Her wails continued unabated despite what I thought was my best soothing daddy voice.

I wished she understood that I was going to the kitchen to fix her bottle and that everything would be fine, I told myself. Maybe someday she will understand that her mommy and daddy are always here for her and that we will always take care of her.

As I inched along in the darkness, I stepped on a plastic Lego toy, leaving a kind of waffle print on the ball of my right foot. Now both of my feet throbbed. I groped along the wall and slowly shuffled in the moon-lit darkness to find the light switch, and after what seemed an eternal moment, due to Anorah's crying, turned on the light and squinted to find the kitchen sink, a bottle of liquid hand soap, and a small hand towel. Turning the water on to wash my hands, I found it frigid and washed quickly. Outside the confines of our small wooden home, the roaring sounds of the wind rudely reminded me that I was in Michigan in the heart of winter. I was glad that my family was safe inside, not feeling the effects of the minus 25-degree wind chill.

Opening the refrigerator door, I spied two plastic milk containers partially hidden behind the Tupperware set containing last night's leftover dinner of meatloaf, macaroni and cheese, and broccoli. Moving the Tupperware aside, I grabbed the wrong milk. Anorah still drank whole milk, while Lori and I had switched to skim. Through squinted eyes I took care to grab the right milk this time. I quickly opened the cupboard only to find that there were no bottles. Anorah seemed to go through a lot of bottles, and I was glad that we had run the dishwasher last night after dinner. Opening the dishwasher, I fumbled around, located a bottle, cap and nipple, and clumsily poured the milk into the bottle, spilling a few drops on the counter and floor. I grabbed a paper napkin, and half-heartedly swiped at the spilled droplets and, mindful of Anorah's continuing wails, was grateful that Lori is a deep sleeper.

With a flick of the light switch in Anorah's room, the bright light momentarily blinded me. Entering Anorah's room, my eyes quickly went to her crimson colored, distorted face. She still looked beautiful I thought, in spite of her crying. She was standing in her crib hanging on to the rails, seemingly inconsolable, as if her entire world had collapsed. Her Peter Rabbit sheets were wrapped around her chubby legs and her pink blankets had bunched up in the corner of the crib. Quickly rushing to Anorah's aid, I told myself that I was making up for the time that I lost when I fumbled about earlier. She eagerly grabbed the bottle that I thrust at her and began sucking down its soothing contents.

The house was instantly quiet. Her face faded from crimson to a subdued shade of pink. The sounds of Anorah slurping milk were the only audible noises, outside of the roaring wind, which seemed even louder in the absence of her crying.

Lifting her gingerly from the crib, I cradled my beloved daughter as if protecting her from the cold world outside, and slowly lowered myself into the antique wicker backed rocking chair, taking care not to move too quickly and disturb her. Sitting there, I noticed the Peter Rabbit mural looking down on me from the wall above the crib. Peter's light blue coat appeared even more faded under the moonlight. Looking up at me with pure love, Anorah's sucking slowed and the bottle drooped from her lips as she fell back asleep. I cradled her tenderly in my arms and watched her sleep, feeling her warm breath on my left arm. I felt proud and protective.

After a few minutes I gingerly pushed myself up from the rocking chair using the armrest. Walking quietly and slowly across the carpeted floor, I gently laid her down in the crib; tucking her in and being careful to cover her well, and to make sure that the curtains were drawn. I tiptoed from her bedroom and returned to the kitchen where I placed her half-full bottle in the refrigerator.

Heading back to bed, I flicked off the lights, leaving only the pale rays of the half moon glimmering through the blinds to guide my footsteps. Carefully pulling back the sheets so as not to disturb Lori, I eased myself under the warm covers, taking special care not to brush her with my ice cold feet. Her quiet breathing assured me that she was sleeping, and I exhaled a sigh of comfort at having such a loving wife. I snuggled in to go back to sleep.

"John, what was wrong?" Lori asked, breaking me loose from my thoughts and turning to face me.

"Oh. I thought you were asleep. Did I wake you?"

"No, I was lying here resting. What was wrong with Anorah? Is she sleeping?"

"Yes," I whispered. "She fell asleep immediately after her bottle. I think she was just hungry. Boy, was she wailing. I guess in her little mind she must have thought her world was falling apart and nothing could fix it."

"Oh, Okay, good night."

As we both lay there, I silently pondered the wonder of our daughter and the joy she brings into our life. Sleep seemed to have overtaken Lori when I couldn't contain my excitement and I gently nudged her awake even though I knew that she had to get up for work in a few hours.

"Lori, Lori, wake up." I implored softly.

"Huh, what John, what? Is Anorah okay?"

"She's fine honey, I'm sorry about waking you, but I'm so excited about a thought that I had I just did not want to wait until morning and lose it!"

"Okay, let's hear it," she replied sleepily. Lori has long been tolerant of my tendency to share ideas at any time.

"Well, while she was crying, I was thinking: if she only knew, if she only understood that her Daddy was fixing her bottle and everything is going to be fine; if she understood that, then she wouldn't be so devastated. And then I got to thinking, now don't think this is silly, okay?"

"Okay," she replied.

"I sometimes ponder about the mystery of God and what His plan is for us. I occasionally wonder about this gift of life and why bad things happen sometimes. We often feel our world is falling apart, just like Anorah might have felt while I was fixing her bottle. She had no idea what I was doing. She only knew she was hungry and that her world, as she knows it, was falling apart."

"That's true," Lori agreed.

"You know, honey, I wonder if when we think our world is falling apart and life has taken a bad turn and we are inconsolable, if God is in the kitchen fixing our bottle so to speak. Maybe, just as we take care of Anorah, God is taking care of us. In the same way that she was unaware of my efforts to fix her bottle, maybe we are unaware of God's efforts to take care of us. Perhaps our view of God and His magnificent plan is even more limited than Anorah's view of us. What do you think?"

Lori lay there silently, and I thought that maybe she had fallen back asleep or had simply decided not to respond out of politeness to protect my feelings. I was slowly warming up from my trip out to fix Anorah' s bottle and felt slightly overwhelmed with the thought of God fixing my bottle.

Peace came over me as I thought about this metaphor and the notion that all of the times throughout my life I was troubled,

God really was in the kitchen fixing my bottle and bottles for people all over the world. As the room grew more silent and peaceful, I considered the nice things that come out of kitchens such as brownies and Christmas and Thanksgiving dinners. The kitchen is a place of sustenance and nurturance, and the thought of God in the kitchen fixing my bottle seemed so right to me.

"Lori, you think it's silly about God being in the kitchen, don't you?"

"No," she replied. "I think it's a beautiful thought and it gives me great comfort. You're right, God is in the kitchen. Thank you for sharing it. I'll think of it often when I'm troubled. You've given me a great gift."

We fell asleep in each other's arms, both of us secure in the vision that God is in the kitchen fixing our bottle.

****

I can hardly count the number of times that I've felt troubled about events in my life that I thought were negative such as losing a job, losing my wallet and credit card, minor health related issues, or other things like car problems. Sometimes these things worked out well, and sometimes not. Yet, when it is all said and done, I've learned to develop a sense of calm and sanguine nature about how my life evolves with the belief that God is in the kitchen and He is taking care of us.

SMILE AND SHE'LL SMILE BACK

The greatest discovery of my generation is that human beings can alter their lives by altering their attitudes of mind.
~ William James

"I feel good, do, do, do, do, do, do, do, like I knew that I would now, do, do, do, do, do, do, do. I feel good, do, do, do, do, do, like I knew that I would, do, do, do, do, do, do, so good, so good, I love you, do, do, do, do, do, ah!"

Gradually, Anorah's crying subsided as I continued to hold her closely and sang her favorite song—James Brown's "I Feel Good." I sang it as though I were in front of 20,000 screaming, rabid, excited fans in Madison Square Garden, not just one screaming 6-month-old baby girl. The Godfather of Soul's signature song, reverberating with energy, passion, and soul, seemed to be the one way to soothe Anorah's crying jags when a bottle would not suffice. The pediatrician had informed Lori and I that Anorah was a bit colicky. We both tried everything that we could think of over the past week to calm her, when I stumbled upon "I Feel Good."

Since it was only 10 a.m. and she had just awakened, Anorah was still wearing her fuzzy Pooh Bear pajamas with yellow and pink stripes and footies. I'd already changed her diaper, given her a bottle, walked her and answered the phone about five times from various solicitors trying hard to get their hands on our money. Each hung up the phone without success.

Lori had recently returned to teaching school, and I was balancing Mr. Mom duties and consulting, although my primary role at the moment was to stay home and nurture Anorah, which as any stay-at-home mother, or father will tell you, is not only a full-time job, it is the only job. My creativity in feeding and nurturing her developing brain was sometimes taxed, but quitting was not an option.

While carrying her around the house and singing "I Feel Good," I noticed that Anorah seemed fixated with the family pictures hung montage-style, in single brown oak frames, on the hallway wall. Showing her pictures of Lori's family might stimulate her mind, I thought, and it might give us both something to do during the long day. "That's Grandma, and Granddad, and Uncle Jim, and Uncle Reed, and Aunt Amy, and Uncle Scott and Aunt Mary with your great-aunt Pat. Look, there are your cousins Reed and John. And there is your great-grandma, Nana. That's your Granddad's mom." She smiled as if she knew who and what I was showing her.

She soon tired of the pictures, so I carried her into the living room where I grabbed the sports page from the *Detroit Free Press*. As Anorah snuggled into my lap, I settled back into a white overstuffed chair to read about the latest baseball off-season trades in the *Free Press* and speculation about whether the Tigers should remodel venerated and historic Tiger Stadium, or build a new stadium.

Anorah soon fell asleep, no doubt as bored with the Tigers as I was. I held her in my lap for awhile, listening to rhythmic breathing and watching her stomach rise and fall with each new breath. Momentarily, I gingerly raised myself out of the chair, although it was not easy holding her in one hand and pushing myself up with the other. I slowly and carefully walked to her bedroom, watching out for her stuffed bunny on the floor and the miscellaneous other toys such as her pink four-wheel-drive toy truck and her dark blue toy piano with the missing key, so that we did not trip. I promised myself that I'd clean up while Anorah was napping.

I gently put her in her crib, covered her up with the Peter Rabbit sheets, and tiptoed from the room. It was now nearly 12 noon. Although I was hungry, more than that, I, too, was sleepy and crawled into our bed, pulled the covers over my head, and instantly dozed off, forgetting to put away her toys. Fixing her bottle in the middle of the night is hard business.

Forty-five minutes later or so, I awoke and planned the rest of the day. My plan looked like this: Watch Anorah, feed Anorah, amuse Anorah, and, of course, change her diapers. Anorah's nap ended much too quickly for me, and she announced her dissatisfaction of finding herself alone in her crib by crying up a storm of tears. At moments like that, I had learned, a bottle of formula and my hugs and attention were the magic elixir required for calming her. She drank the formula for about 12 minutes, and her visage of contentment was a joy to both of us. She did not drink all of the formula, so I returned the half-full bottle to the refrigerator, and had visions of having to break into another rendition of "I Feel Good" to quiet her crying. To my great relief, Anorah remained calm. Wondering what to do next, I stumbled upon a lesson in social skills.

We walked down the hall past the family pictures on the wall and took a left turn into Anorah's bedroom. While she focused on the painted Beatrix Potter mural that we had commissioned by a local artist prior to Anorah's birth, I searched for something to amuse her before her brief attention span caused her to lose patience with me.

I picked her up around her waist beneath her tiny arms and gently lifted her so that she was chest high on me. Together we faced the tan-hued wicker-framed mirror hung on her pale yellow wall. She seemed disinterested as I bounced her up and down, made funny faces and noises, danced around on one foot, and finally smiled into the mirror. "Smile, and she'll smile back," I said hopefully. "Smile, and she'll smile back," I offered one more time, knowing it was unlikely she would change her expression since she didn't yet speak or understand language—or so I thought.

I was about ready to give up when to my great astonishment Anorah started giggling at herself in the mirror. Her smile was nearly as wide as her face, and her joy filled up the room as it surely does the soul and heart of a proud father. It must have worked, I told myself. "Smile, and she'll smile back," I encouraged. We spent the next fifteen or so minutes giggling and cooing at each other in the mirror, our joy only heightened by Lori's return from teaching. Lori rushed in to hug and kiss Anorah in a way that transcends love.

"Hi, sweetie, did you miss Momma today? Momma missed you, honey, and I am so glad to be home with you and Daddy." Anorah cooed and smiled back and for now, at least in our family, all seemed right with the world.

The evening went by quickly. Before we knew it, dinner—a frozen lasagna, and small salad, had been served and eaten. The dishes were rinsed, and put into the dishwasher, and the table was cleaned and the floor swept. Anorah was bathed, put into her favorite pajamas, rocked and read to by her mommy, and was now asleep in Lori's arms. After putting Anorah to bed, Lori came back into the living room eager to spend time with me and talk about the day. She sat down on the couch and with a devilish smile asked if I would rub her sore feet.

I placed her left foot on my right thigh and began gently massaging along the arch; "Anorah seemed really happy when I returned home, giggling, cooing, and smiling," Lori said through a sigh of satisfaction as my fingers traced up and down on the ball of her foot. "What were you guys doing?"

"Smiling at each other," I replied and repositioned myself to accommodate her right foot. "We were playing a mirror game."

"A mirror game. What's a mirror game?" she asked with closed eyes.

"It's a game that seemed to really hold her attention and got her giggling after she awoke from her nap. I was trying to find something to do with her, you know, keep her amused, and at the same time maybe teach her something, when I stumbled across the mirror game. We walked into her bedroom and I showed her her face in the mirror and said, 'smile, and she'll smile back,' a couple of times, when all of a sudden she started looking into the mirror and giggling at herself. You should've seen it, Lori. It was pure joy for both of us."

Lori gave me an amused grin as she stretched out her toes. "You know, John, that's interesting. I was talking to Jenny, one of my students, who was complaining that no one ever talks to her or tries to make friends with her and that she is lonely. I asked her if she ever reaches out to other students, or initiates conversations, or invites anyone to sit with her at lunch. She replied, no, not really. She said that no one ever did that for her, so why should she do that for him or her? I told her that if she wanted people to talk to her and be her friend, she needed to initiate conversations and reach out to others first. I told her that sometimes it is scary and risky to invite someone to hang out with her, but no risk, no reward."

I sat there silently for a moment. "How did Jenny respond to that?" I appreciated how we were able to change the subject of our conversation without really changing the content of the conversation.

"She responded with some fear and trepidation, and a really negative attitude, but I think she is more frustrated and scared than negative. It's like that mirror, John," Lori said as if she had just read my mind, and was answering a question that was never asked. "Anorah was only going to be able to see a smile in the mirror if she smiled into it. Or, in your words, 'smile, and she'll smile back'. Jenny needs to smile and others will smile back. That's all any of us really need to do. Reach out to others and they will reach back. Help others and they'll help back. I will share this with Jenny and the rest of the class tomorrow!"

"Or," I interjected, "as the Beatles once sang, 'and in the end, the love you take is equal to the love you make.'"

****

Anorah's lesson to me, "smile, and she'll smile back," was, of course, unintended by her. But it continues to have a great influence on my life. That seemingly simple lesson reminds me to be confident and outgoing when entering a group of strangers, to smile when meeting Lori after a long tough day, or to be friendly and courteous when exiting a check out-lane in the midst of a crowd of impatient shoppers eager to get home. "Smile, and she'll smile back," is not only a fun game to play in front of the mirror with Anorah; it is tantamount to the Golden Rule and suggests that we all benefit if we treat others as we want to be treated. Plus, it is a fun way for me to live my life, which is after all about attitudes and action.

AVERAGE ICE WATER

When you're average, you're just as close to the bottom as you are the top.

~ Source Unknown ~

"Honey, it's Friday night and we've all had a hard week. How about if we treat ourselves and go out for dinner?" Lori asked with a smile that suggested that this was not a request, but more like a directive.

"Well, okay," I replied with noticeable hesitation. Eating dinner in a public place with Anorah, who was then 3 years old, can be challenging. Like most three-year-olds, she is energetic, curious, and seems to be interested in nearly anything but her food when she is in a restaurant. But, I was tired, too, from the long workweek, and eating out as a family sounded fun, and a nice break from the toils of the week.

I suggested a nearby restaurant known for its fast service, mediocre food and faux Italian atmosphere. Lori quickly agreed and off we went, but not before Anorah sprinted away, her little legs churning and her arms flailing in search of her pets. Any pet would do, I suspected. Lori chased her around the corner of the house and found her squealing with delight as she petted her Black Labrador, Magic. Magic's tail wagged with almost hysteric delight, as Anorah's hands, almost equally hysteric, stroked and patted his black and graying muzzle. "Magic, Magic, my baby, how are you?" She cooed at him with clear adoration. Of course, Magic was not only wagging his tail at nearly the speed of light, or so it seemed, he was returning Anorah's cooing in his dog-like way with grunts, moans and head gyrations.

"They make quite a pair, don't you think, John? They almost seem as if they are actually talking to each other," Lori giggled to me.

"Of course, I noted with a smile, our dog, our daughter and such obvious delight, it almost beats dinner; but, it's time to go, so why don't we wrap up this love fest, and head for the restaurant."

I almost pleaded since these petting sessions sometimes become almost near marathons of pet-love. With great persuasion by Lori and a small bribe by me (I promised Anorah an ice cream cone after dinner, which was followed by a disapproving, but amused, look by Lori), Anorah agreed to leave her beloved Magic behind, but not before one last hug and a doggy treat.

Lori gathered Anorah up into her arms and strapped her into her car seat, being careful to make sure that the seat was secure and that all of her straps properly fit and were buckled. Meanwhile, I fed Magic his dry rice and lamb dog food in his old scratched plastic dog bowl. His tail wagged nearly as much as when he was playing with Anorah. Anorah quickly forgot about Magic and seemed delighted to be out on the town.

"It's starting to rain, John, is there an umbrella in the Jeep?"

"No, I'm afraid not; I forgot to put it back into the car after I cleaned it out yesterday. Sorry," I replied. The heavy rains tapped, tapped, and tapped upon the Jeep in a way that was soothing and almost hypnotic.

"It's just like a giant car wash, Momma!" Anorah exclaimed with joy. Meanwhile, the Jeep splashed through the temporary mud puddles created by the rains on the blacktopped two-lane road. "Water wings" created by the Jeep driving through the expanding puddles splashed nearly up to the windows, causing Anorah to giggle with delight. We finally arrived at the restaurant safe, sound, hungry, and muddy.

Pulling up as close to the front door as I could, Lori and Anorah were able to make a short run for a long green canvas canopy that led to the front door of the restaurant. I was lucky to find a nearby parking spot, and I managed to avoid much of the downpour as I, too, ran to the dryness of the canopy and into the restaurant.

"Wow, I'm glad I found that spot," I commented as I wiped raindrops from my left arm. "And we are really lucky because it looks as though we beat the dinner crowd. We should be able to get our order in quickly."

The hostess seated us after only about a two-minute wait. One of our private jokes about this restaurant is my request to be seated by a window overlooking the lake. The first time we ate there, with our friends Mike and Vicki and their toddler son Alex, the ground was covered with snow. For reasons unknown to me, I thought that the snow-covered flat farmland was a frozen ice and snow-covered lake in winter. Needless to say, my disappointment was palpable that first spring to find it was only a hay field and not a bucolic blue wonderland dotted with sail boats that I might enjoy during my dinner.

Sitting down, Lori and I scanned the menu and opted for a simple dinner of spaghetti with tomato sauce and a side salad with croutons, tomatoes, cucumbers and blue cheese dressing. Anorah demanded Chicken McNuggets, even though we were not at McDonalds. She typically asks for Chicken McNuggets "with catsup." She settled for the chicken strips. Dinner came quickly, and since it was late and neither of us had eaten for seven hours or so, our salad and spaghetti were quickly gone. Anorah was rather deliberate in her eating, although I felt grateful, since she stayed at our table and was not running around the restaurant making new friends. Lori and I relaxed and watched while Anorah alternately ate and played both with her food and the crayons that the restaurant brought for her.

"Lori, we've really been here a long time, don't you think?" I was starting to feel impatient with Anorah's dawdling. "We finished our dinners a long time ago and have been here so long that the ice has melted in my water and gotten warm."

"I know, honey," Lori replied, gentle as always, although I could tell that she was tired, too. "Anorah is a little girl and is easily distracted. I really want her to finish her dinner. She hasn't been eating well lately, you know, and she seems to like her meal tonight. Besides," Lori brightened, "she's merely enjoying the ambiance of the restaurant. Look at it that way."

"Okay honey, I smiled in return, but this is starting to resemble one of those three-hour dinners that we experienced in Italy," I remarked with a small measure of impatience. I had found those traditionally long Italian dinners somewhat tedious, and would sometimes go for a walk while Lori visited with new friends.

"Ambiance, what ambiance?" I thought to myself. There really wasn't much in the way of décor, but I decided to look since I am usually in such a rush that I often don't see where I am or where I am going. The inexpensive posters of pasta, loaves of Italian bread, bottles of dark wine, and the leaning tower of Pisa were a genuine, but feeble attempt to create an Italian atmosphere.

"Daddy, Daddy," Anorah squeaked in her sweetest baby tone, quickly interrupting my reverie and increasing interest in the décor. "I'm thirsty. Can I have your water?" Little did I know that I was about to learn another lesson. They seem to come in the most unexpected ways and packages.

"Of course, I replied, but it's warm and may not taste too good."

"Why is it warm, Daddy?" Anorah asked the question in that special three-year-old voice, so soft, sincere and in a way that always melts my heart.

"Well, I replied, my voice rising to my fatherly role, we've been here a long time, and the room temperature is warmer than the ice water. The room is warm and the ice is cold. The warmth in the room caused the ice to melt and now the water and the room are nearly the same temperature."

"Oh," she replied, her soft blue-green eyes glazed over by my explanation. "Can I have your water now?"

Carefully handing Anorah the glass, I cautioned her to use both hands so she would not spill it. She took a big gulp and announced in one long breath, "You're right, Daddy, it's too warm. Make it cold again and put more ice in it. Okay, Daddy?" I beckoned to a waiter, who seeing my harried daddy look, hurried over and refreshed the warm, half-full glass with cool icy water. Anorah took the glass to her lips. "Now it's cold. Just the way I like it. Thanks, Daddy. Good job. I'm proud of you. How come it got cold again?"

This child is a living game of *Jeopardy*, only with much tougher questions, I thought to myself. But then again most children are very curious. "The waiter put fresh water in the glass with ice, and the ice made the water cold again," I explained.

"So now it's colder than the room, huh, Daddy?" Anorah offered through a broad smile that signaled her new understanding.

"You got it, Sweetie. How did you get so smart?" I asked.

"I just am," Anorah responded matter-of-factly, then returned to toying with the remaining chicken strips and French fries on her plate. "Can I have my dish of ice cream now, Daddy? You promised," Anorah implored.

"Of course. Look, it's on its way now," I pointed to the waiter who must have some sort of ESP, I decided.

"I've got a niece about that age, he smiled and looked at me knowingly, and she just loves ice cream; I'll bet you do, too, honey," he smiled at Anorah.

"Of course, everybody loves ice cream," she said nearly incredulously. Consumed with help from Mom and Dad, the ice cream was quickly eaten and Anorah left the restaurant full of ice cream and happy, as did Dad.

The rain had stopped, but the roads were still wet from the earlier downpour, and on this late spring evening, the smell of fresh cut grass, plowed fields and spring renewal was so present it was almost the only thing, except for the stars. The stars were so bright; they seemed as though they were dancing on our windshield with us on this lonely country road, and not millions of miles away in the distant sky. The short ride home was silent, but sensorially stunning in a way that ignites your senses and makes you glad to be alive. Anorah quickly fell asleep and missed nature's show.

Upon returning home, I opened the garage door, the dog barked, the cat cried and Lori deftly removed Anorah from her car seat, carried her into the house, removed her clothes, and put on her pajamas in what seemed like one effortless motion. I took the dog for a quick walk around the neighborhood. When I returned, Lori was comfortably settled in an easy chair reading *The Rainmaker, a* John Grisham novel that she had received as a birthday present from her brother Jim, who is also an attorney. I scooped *up The Alchemist,* by Paulo Coelho. I have read this book at least 15 times and yet each reading is an enlightening experience, and I find new ways to look at the world.

A soft breeze blew through the open window in the family room, and I felt both greatly at peace and inspired. As I scanned the words of the book, I found myself thinking about, of all things, ice water.

"Hey, Lori," I interrupted her reading, something I think she's gotten used to. "We're just like ice water."

Looking up at me from the book with a combination of bemusement and annoyance, Lori said, "What does that mean, John?"

"Think about it," I responded, encouraged by her look. "No matter how you frame it, that ice water in the restaurant was different."

"Different than what, John?" Lori asked.

"Well, the temperature of the ice water was not average, at least when it was fresh. After we sat there for a while, the water got warm and stale. Then after the glass was filled up with more ice and water, it was exceptional in its own way, because it was much colder than the surrounding room. For water to be different, exceptional, it must constantly be replenished or else it becomes the same temperature as the rest of the room; in other words, average. And in being replenished, it must remove some of the existing water to make room for the new colder water and ice."

"Okay, John, where are you going with this?" I heard her underlying impatience, so I spoke quickly.

"Just like a glass of water that needs to be replenished with new ice and fresh water in order to be cold, people must continually shed outmoded ideas, bad habits, selfishness, and other personal shortcomings and continually renew themselves through new experiences, new ideas, new information, or simply by stretching themselves beyond their comfort zone. In order to reach our potential, grow as people, be happy and be able to look back upon our lives with satisfaction, we must renew ourselves constantly. Just like the ice water turned warm, unless we renew ourselves, we, too, run the risk of being average. Or even worse, we can become disillusioned and disconnected from society, our family and even ourselves." I paused for effect and gave her a big smile. "That's how we're like ice water!"

"Oh," she replied, closing her book and turning her attention to me. "Tell me more."

****

Thoreau wrote "the mass of men lead lives of quiet desperation." Perhaps some of that desperation comes from our failure to appreciate our ability to choose and to accept the responsibility to grow and to renew ourselves.

If we fail to renew ourselves, to grow, to learn to recreate ourselves we are simply making our own early grave. The metaphor of renewing our ice water by removing stale water and melted ice, and replacing it with new ice and water suggests renewal, invigoration, and the opportunity to cease being average. We can then constantly stay productive, fresh and are best able to serve our God, our family, our community and ourselves. After all, no one wants to be average and I suspect that God, too, wants us to renew ourselves.

FOLLOW YOUR BLISS

Twenty years from now you will be more disappointed by the things that you didn't do than by the ones you did do. So throw off the bowlines. Sail away from the safe harbor. Catch the trade winds in your sails. Explore. Dream. Discover.

—Mark Twain

"Daddy, Daddy, come play with me! Daddy, Daddy, let's play! Come on, Daddy, please," Anorah pleaded enthusiastically, her tiny hands yanking at my pants leg.

"What should we do?" I asked, hoping she would choose to read a book or something equally passive since I was somewhat tired from working in the yard, which although I enjoy, is tiresome at times.

"We'll play hide and seek, Daddy, that's what we'll do. Now you go hide and I'll find you. Okay, Daddy, go hide now, Okay?"

Adoring her the way I do, I had little choice and dutifully ran off to find an easily discovered hiding place so that she could find me and I could act surprised when she did. Hearing her count slowly from one to ten, I headed for the dining room and hugged the far wall knowing that Anorah would find me quickly. In a matter of seconds, she burst into the room.

"Daddy, Daddy, I found you!" she squealed with equal parts of delight and triumph. "I found you, Daddy; now it's my turn to hide," she announced through a broad smile on her cherubic little face. I quickly turned my face to the dining room wall, and as I do, I glimpse the famous Michelangelo print of God reaching His hand to Adam. We saw this beautifully symbolic representation of God's love for man at a local furniture store, fell in love with it immediately, and bought it on the spot. We then purchased more of Michelangelo's prints while visiting the Sistine Chapel and also hung them in the dining room. The pictures create a very spiritual aura.

I counted loudly and slowly to ten: "One, two, three, four."

"Come on, Daddy, find me! Hurry up and count!" Anorah whooped. "Come find me!"

"Five, six, seven, eight, nine, ten," I hurriedly finished counting.

Dropping my hands from my eyes, I walked briskly through the arched doorway in the dining room and into the living room. Anorah lay length-wise beneath the oval coffee table, her torso hidden, but her bare feet clearly visible. I pretended to search for her as if I could not locate her hiding place. I looked underneath the dining room table, and with a loud voice called out, "Anorah, are you here?" I then looked in the kitchen cupboards, underneath the comforter on the already made bed and finally in the coat closet in the living room. Feigning frustration, I called out: "Lori, I can't find Anorah. Do you know where she is? She's really hidden well this time."

"Gee, I don't know where she is either. I wonder where she could be," Lori chimed in playfully.

"I'll keep looking," I announced as I exited the living room.

Anorah could no longer contain her excitement and blurted out, "I'm here, you silly! I'm here! You couldn't find me, could you, Daddy? I'm under the table."

"Anorah, you hide so well. I never would have found you in a million years. How do you do that?"

"I just do, Daddy," she replied in a tone of confidence that I find delightful.

"Let's do something else, Daddy. How about if we put together a puzzle? I'll go get one right now!" she offered as she skipped off, nearly tripping over the burgundy ottoman that sits near the overstuffed easy chair.

"Be careful, honey," I cautioned. "Please watch where you're going."

"Okay, Daddy, I will," she replied as she almost immediately returned to the living room with her favorite Beauty and the Beast puzzle in hand. I wonder to myself why she is so quick to find her puzzle, but can never find her shoes when it's time to go to daycare? No matter, I guess it's just a parent's lament. The contents of the box were dumped onto the white living room carpet in what looked like a million pieces. An involuntary sigh escaped my lips as I reached underneath the green couch for a stray piece that had cartwheeled its way into hiding.

"Look, Daddy, I got these two pieces to fit together, the yellow ones. I think this is Belle's dress 'cause her dress is yellow. Don't you think so, Daddy?"

"Of course, you're right, that is Belle's dress." I marveled how quickly a three-year-old could put together a puzzle. Concentrating on the task at hand, we slowly created a picture out of the tangle of pieces. A colorful scene of Belle in her swirling yellow gown and the Beast in his blue suit gliding over the wooden dance floor soon took shape.

Delighted with the finished product, Anorah could not contain her enthusiasm and blurted out: "Look, Daddy! Look what we did. Belle and the Beast are dancing. I wish I could dance with somebody. Maybe we could dance, Daddy, okay? Why don't we dance right now?"

"Maybe Mommy will dance with you?" I offered hopefully, telling myself that I would like to take a momentary break.

"No, Daddy, I want to dance with you! You're just like the Beast and I am like Belle!"

"Just like the Beast. You think your father looks like the Beast?"

"No, silly, we're just pretending. Now come dance with me, okay, right now." I twirled her around as we sang the theme song from the movie. She asked me to call her Belle and she continued to refer to me as the Beast. Round and round the living room we went. Anorah's levels of energy and enthusiasm were seemingly unlimited. I was ready to call it quits when Lori finally came to my rescue by telling Anorah it was time to take her bath.

"Do I have to wash my hair tonight, Mommy?" she asked, her baby-blue eyes twinkling. "I just washed it last night, you know."

"Oh, I suppose not, Anorah, but we need to get really clean since you went to the carnival this morning," Lori instructed. "Okay, Mommy, let's go take a bath," Anorah agreed and then added: "Will you take a bath with me, Mommy, for just a few minutes, please?"

Fingers intertwined, they skipped out of the room, leaving me a chance to get on the Internet for a few minutes. I logged on to the computer and went directly to Yahoo, the Internet search portal, to see how my stocks had ended the day. With some dismay I noted that Leapnet, a small holding in my small portfolio had, once again, gone down. Stopping to listen for a moment, I could hear Anorah's laughter from upstairs as it cascaded down the stairway into the living room. Lori was laughing, too, and I could imagine both of them in the tub splashing around and playing with Anorah's toys.

After 15 minutes or so, Anorah came padding down the stairs. I saw her slowly descending the white carpet covered stairs and marveled at how beautiful she looked, her fuzzy pink and yellow striped Winnie the Pooh pajamas looking more elegant than any evening gown ever had.

"Daddy, Daddy, will you read me a story? Will you read me Calvin and Hobbs?" Anorah is a big fan of Calvin and Hobbs, the comic strip by Bill Waterman, and I welcomed her to my lap for a few minutes of reading.

"It sounds like you and Mommy were really having fun up there," I commented.

"Mommy kept splashing me, Daddy. It was so much fun. I got her wet too, Daddy. Now can you read me Calvin and Hobbs?"

Anorah crawled into my lap, snuggled close against my chest and we both laughed at the high jinks and irreverence of Calvin and Hobbs. The time sped by much too quickly until it was time for her to go to bed.

"Olay Punkin," it's time to go meet Mr. Sandman," Lori called out.

"Mr. Sandman! Not him again, where is he?" Anorah asked playfully. Lori gave Anorah her vitamin, brushed her teeth, and tucked her beneath the sheets. Anorah went directly to sleep, which is not always the case. Lori returned from Anorah's bedroom, sat next to me, and through a sigh of relief announced: "She went to sleep easily tonight. I must have worn her out in the bathtub."

"She sure was laughing," I observed. "I could hear you all the way down here. I really enjoyed listening to the two of you being happy together. It was almost as if you were right next to me."

"We were —in spirit," Lori offered brightly.

"You know, it seems as though all she did today was laugh and smile. In fact, it seems most of the time she's laughing and smiling. I guess when you're a toddler with loving parents you don't have a care in the world and so you can laugh and smile all the time."

"Yeah, you're right, John. She really doesn't have much to worry about, unless it's getting another Barbie doll. But I have noticed something else."

"What's that?"

"She's always happy because she's always doing exactly what she wants to do. She's doing what self-development guru Wayne Dyer is always writing and talking about: following her bliss. She's always following her bliss, so of course she's happy," Lori observed as she lay her head on my shoulder and placed her hand softly over my heart. "Most of us spend our days doing someone else's bidding, living someone else's dreams, and coming and going on someone else's clock. I think it was Thoreau who noted that most men lead lives of quiet desperation, I guess because we don't follow our bliss, don't do what we want, and do the bidding of others. Anorah is a child, and of, course she doesn't have to do that. She does what makes her happy."

"That reminds me of something the songwriter and singer Harry Chapin said in one of his songs, or maybe it was just on one of his albums," I offered. "Anyway, he said his grandfather once told him about good tired and bad tired. Bad tired is when you fight someone else's battles and while you may even win some of them, you know in your heart that you did not fight your own battles, on your own terms, for your own passions. Rather, you did someone else's bidding. Good tired, on the other hand is when you fight your own battles on your own terms, and even if you are dog tired, and even if you lost, it is a tired that makes you feel proud." "Well," I laughed, I guess I would say that Anorah is good tired! How about you?"

****

My thoughts went to my own life. Like most people, I would rather be good tired than bad tired. And like many people I have failed to follow my bliss. So it seems that I spend too much of my day being and feeling bad tired. Maybe I should learn yet another lesson from Anorah and find a way to follow my bliss, be good tired, and to fight my own battles.

Lord knows I've lost a lot of them, but each one seemed to leave me a little stronger, a little braver and, I think, a little better person. A universal truth lies within each of us, within each of our hearts and souls: knowing our bliss, is not difficult. But having the courage to follow our bliss, however, that's another matter entirely. Yet, as Mark Twain reminds us, our regrets will come not from following our bliss, and perhaps stumbling along the way, but from not following our bliss, from not taking chances, and from not living out our life's dreams. In the end, our regrets will not be that we took a chance and had a setback, but that we took no risk and achieved nothing at all, or very little, that we desired.

MR. POTTY PANTS

Comparisons are odious.

~ Fourteenth Century Saying ~

The 30-mile drive along Interstate 94 to Kalamazoo from Battle Creek, Michigan, went slowly on the warm, humid, and mostly cloudy August late afternoon. Big semi-trucks full of cargo were choking the highway and slowing traffic, a stalled car on the side of the road caused traffic to slow even further, and the police had pulled over yet another car. Plus, it was Friday afternoon and everyone was eager to go home.

Still, in spite of all of the need for focus in these busy and dangerous conditions, I drove my blue Ford Taurus nearly indifferently to the responsibilities of navigating roads and streets and sharing the roads with other cars. I had just left a staff meeting at work where annual raises were discussed and where notices of raise levels were confidentially distributed. To my dismay and near fury, I was given a smaller raise than I had expected or thought fair, especially since raises are based upon perceived performance.

My thoughts were assaulted by negative self-talk, which was a habit left over from my days in foster care and children's institutions when I literally had to fight to survive. "It's not fair!" I told myself. I had such conviction about my position and vigor that, like the character in Edgar Allan Poe's short story, "The Tell-Tale Heart," who is afraid that others will hear his heart beating with fear and guilt, I was afraid others might hear my inner, unspoken talk. "Others got bigger raises than I did. I worked really hard, had several articles published, gave dozens of speeches on youth development, attended all of the staff meetings, and all-in-all fulfilled my responsibilities in a superior manner. I know my job, perform it well, and deserve better."

I was really on a roll with my self-talk. "I know personnel evaluation. I have a doctorate in evaluation. I was the lead designer for the personnel evaluation and selection process for the Marine Corps, and I knew how to advise the Corps to select and promote their few good men. Just who do they think they are using that substandard personnel evaluation system to justify not giving me a bigger raise?"

Totally embroiled in negative thoughts, I nearly failed to brake at a four-way stop after I had gotten off the highway, and had to swerve to miss a white Cadillac driven by a balding but courtly senior citizen accompanied by a white-haired woman who was likely his wife. There was a huge cloud of dust and small gravel flying in my wake as I pulled back onto the road after going momentarily into the gravel shoulder alongside a cornfield after I swerved to miss them. The elderly couple seemed close enough to touch me, and their eyes locked onto mine in a visual dance of fear.

"Whew, I thought to myself, I am really lucky that no one got hurt. My racing heart slowly returned to its normal beat. At least I had the presence of mind to wear my seat belt," I thought to myself.

Paying better attention to my driving after my near mishap, I slowed down and made a sharp right turn onto the cracked and crumbling concrete driveway to Anorah's daycare center, which is in a small white bungalow house owned by a grandmotherly type whom Anorah adores. Stopping the car, unbuckling my seat belt, and putting the transmission into park, I took a few seconds to compose myself and made it a priority to revert back to my daddy role.

As I entered the fenced-in yard, I stepped over a pink plastic tricycle, a green sandbox shovel, and a stuffed purple and green Barney toy on my way to a barren lawn inside of a chain-link fenced-in area. I don't usually pick up Anorah. Lori normally performs this duty, but that day I was subbing since she had a late meeting at school. It is wonderful to pick up Anorah since she is almost always absurdly enthusiastic about my arrival. As soon as she spotted me, she rushed headlong in my direction, hugged my legs and said: "Daddy, Daddy, pick me up!"

"How's my girl?"

"Okay, Daddy. Can we go now?" I swung her up into my arms and she wrapped her tiny hands around my neck and burrowed her head into my chest. We were one, my precious daughter and I, and each stride toward the car reminded me to savor every step. My negative self-talk and self-preoccupation were instantly replaced by total love.

"Daddy, Daddy, it's not fair!" Anorah exclaimed as I strapped her into the blue car safety seat.

"What's not fair, Anorah?"

"Well, Daddy, Carrie gets to poop in her pants and I don't," Anorah proclaimed, her lower lip quivering ever so slightly.

Anorah was potty trained and a few months older than her friend Carrie who was in daycare with her. I was momentarily puzzled and speechless, which is an unusual occurrence for me. Finally, after I got a chance to compose myself, I responded.

"Anorah, Mommy and I are so proud of you because you are a big girl and big girls go potty in the potty chair. Besides, honey, why would you want to go potty in your pants anyhow?" I responded confidently, thinking my answer was sufficient for a three-year-old. Then she threw me a curve.

"But, Daddy, when I go potty, you or Mom say 'nice job', but that's all you say. Going potty in the potty-chair is such hard work and pooping in my pants is so easy, so maybe I should just poop in my pants, Daddy! It's not fair that I have to work so hard, and Carrie just poops right in her pants."

I pondered her observation, and on the face of it, or what the lawyers call *primae facie* evidence, she had a good point. After all, why should one child be able to poop in their pants and the other not? "I'd like to see that theory argued in a court of law", I thought to myself. In spite of what I thought was pretty sound logic, I didn't want to say anything so fast or thoughtless that I wouldn't give her a truly fatherly answer. I decided not to start the car yet, as I didn't want to repeat my earlier mistake of not focusing on my driving.

My reverie was interrupted with Anorah again loudly proclaiming: "It's not fair!"

"Anorah," I answered, "you are a big girl. Right now it doesn't seem fair, but you are able to go in the potty and only big girls do that, while babies still go in their diapers. You don't even wear diapers, do you?"

"No, that would be silly, I'm a big girl!" she fired back defiantly.

"Good. Then you don't want to go potty in your pants?"

"No. Don't ask me that again. I'm a big girl. Can we go home and see Mommy now?"

"Of course." I was glad that another small parenting crisis had been averted.

The drive home was much more focused for me and much less hazardous for other drivers than was my drive to get Anorah. This time, I paid attention to the other cars on the road, was very aware of stop signs and stop lights, and even drove within the legal speed limit. Still, we got home ahead of Lori, so I spent a few minutes making macaroni and cheese for Anorah and fixing turkey sandwiches with a side of cole slaw, potato chips and a pickle for Lori and me. Upon Lori's return a few minutes later, our light dinner was quickly eaten and the rest of the evening was devoted to reading to Anorah, watching the cartoon Rugrats with Anorah and eating a snack. Tonight's snack consisted of "Moose Tracks," which is a vanilla ice cream liberally filled with a delicious dark chocolate. It's her favorite snack.

Finally, Lori put her to bed with yet another storybook, which happened to be, coincidentally enough, *Once Upon A Potty*, a book about potty training featuring a little girl about Anorah's age named Prudence. Following Anorah's bedtime, Lori and I finally grabbed a few minutes for us while sitting on the family room couch, drinking diet Cokes, and taking the time to reflect on the day's events. "Anorah told me that she wanted to go potty in her pants," I informed Lori with a smile in my voice.

"What do you mean?" she replied with a note of incredulousness in her voice.

I carefully detailed the earlier conversation in the car. Lori listened intently as she always does when something about Anorah is involved, paused and then laughed. "Well, Dr. Spock," she teased, "it sounds as though you relied on all of your child rearing skills and escaped by the skin of your teeth."

"Yes, I guess I did, sort of," I conceded uncertainly. "I guess we'll just have to see how it turns out." There was momentary silence as I prepared to switch subjects.

"I'm really pretty annoyed about something else," I stated, having waited all evening to release my pent-up frustration regarding how poorly I felt I was treated during the personnel evaluation process. I gave her a blow-by-blow description of the unfairness of it all and how I truly believed I had performed so much better than the performance evaluation reflected. Even though it is the policy of my employer to make as many of the staff performance evaluations as they can fall into the average range, in my mind I was definitely not average, regardless of policy.

Lori listened patiently to my tale of woe and then responded in almost an amused way. "You know, John, I feel bad for you, but you know what, you just want to go potty in your pants."

"Excuse me?" I blurted out in a confused and defiant tone, realizing too late that I might not only wake Anorah but half the neighborhood.

"You just want to go potty in your pants," Lori repeated, a look of mirth dancing in her eyes.

"What do you mean?" I replied, with barely concealed annoyance, starting to realize where she was going and not liking it.

"Well, you told Anorah that she is a big girl and that Carrie isn't ready to go potty in the potty chair. You also told her that while this may not seem fair, it actually is fair because Anorah is potty trained and Carrie is not. It may not seem fair on the surface and from Anorah's perspective it's not, but we know things that Anorah does not know, don't we? We know that Anorah is in a different stage of development than Carrie is and we can see things that she can't see." I continued to listen shifting my position on the couch and feeling a wee bit chagrined.

"Maybe what happened today to you with your personnel evaluation process is the adult equivalent of wanting to take the easy way and wanting things to be fair, when you, I think, know better. It seems to me, she continued, that although the circumstances are different between you and Anorah, the principles are the same and they apply to you. Why do you demand or even expect that things be fair? You told Anorah to accept the sometime unfair nature of life, so I suggest that you hold yourself to the same standard."

"If you look at it from Anorah's perspective, it is unfair that she has to go to the bathroom, pull down her pants, wash her hands, and then watch as another child about her age is catered to. Anorah doesn't see the whole picture, and we can't expect her to, but we have to assure her that what is happening is fair, and I believe that you did a good job of convincing her. Perhaps you are not able to see the entire picture at work either, and maybe there are things going on of which you have no knowledge and may not understand, just like Anorah does not understand why she has to go potty in the potty chair and Carrie goes in her diaper. I don't know what those things are, John, but I'm confident that if you listen to what you told Anorah, you will find peace about your performance evaluation."

I sat silently for a while, giving Lori only a brief and somewhat wry smile. She returned to reading her book and I gazed back at the television to watch the Cleveland Indians playing the New York Yankees on ESPN. But I was not really watching the game. Instead, I was thinking about our conversation and my day. I thought about my good fortune to have a daughter who is a natural teacher and a loving wife to share the wisdom of daily life lessons that sometimes escape all of us when Lori interrupted my reverie.

"Remember that story in the New Testament where Jesus tells of the vineyard owner who pays all of his workers the same, from those workers who started early in the morning, to those who started just before quitting time? Isn't that an example of things not seeming fair? But yet here we have God illustrating to us that not all things are fair or at least don't seem fair. So what do you think of that, Mr. Potty-in-your-pants?" she added with a smile.

Finally, after an upper-deck home run by Jim Thome, first baseman for the Indians, I felt better. I reminded Lori that I love her and how grateful I am for our marriage. Lori flashed me her beautiful smile and responded in her most gentle tone: "John, I love you, too. Thanks for sharing both of your stories. It's funny how even the most mundane events can be turned into a life lesson, isn't it?"

****

It's easy to demand fairness, and to expect that we obtain what we believe to be "our fair share." Still, none of us really knows what our fair share might be, or if we even have a fair share. I know that in spite of my difficult childhood, I've received my fair share and I think someone else's, too. I am here with a loving wife and a beautiful daughter, while so many others don't have anywhere near my good fortune. So in the larger cosmic sense, and in the spirit of *God Is In The Kitchen,* I suspect that we are all getting our fair shares. No matter how much we scream about injustice and seek fairness, just as it was fair for Anorah to use the potty while Carrie went in her pants, I suspect that individually our lives are as fair as they should be.

Finding her Toys

Determine what specific goal you want to achieve. Then dedicate yourself to its attainment with unswerving singleness of purpose, the trenchant zeal of a crusader.

~ Paul J. Meyer ~

"She'll crawl over anything to get to her 'Mr. Bun,' won't she?" Lori observed as she sat in the family room keeping an eye on Anorah, carrying on a conversation with me, and reading a book on educational leadership all at once. I am always amazed by Lori's ability to process multiple activities at one time. She is like a juggler who keeps three or more balls in the air without dropping them. Perhaps this is what makes her such a fine teacher. Skillfully coordinating the efforts of so many diverse students is not a job suited for a one-track mind.

"What are you talking about?" I asked.

"Oh, she just crawled over her yellow and purple plastic riding lion (kind of like a plastic riding horse) and knocked it out of the way as if it wasn't there," Lori noted through a slight chuckle.

"Yeah, you're right, but I don't think it's just 'Mr. Bun' that draws her attention," I countered, expanding on Lori's observations. "It seems as though she pursues everything with the same single-minded focus and determination."

Anorah turned and smiled up at Lori and then turned her gaze to me. She knew we were talking about her. Like most babies, Anorah has never been one to turn away from attention. "I guess I'll start calling her Curly," I remarked.

"Who is Curly?" Lori queried. "Do you mean Curly in the Three Stooges?" she continued with justifiable confusion at my somewhat obscure allusion.

"No." I replied. "Curly is that character from the movie *City Slickers*, played by that famous old actor. I can't think of his name."

"Oh, yeah, I remember now," Lori, replied knowingly. "You mean Jack Palance."

"That's it," I blurted out, "Jack Palance, he's the guy that played Curly."

"So what does Jack Palance, er, Curly have to do with Anorah?" Lori asked as she smiled down at Anorah who had finally retrieved her "Mr. Bun" stuffed animal.

"Well, do you remember the scene where the character played by Billy Crystal asks Curly the secret of life; and Curly replies '**one thing**.' Billy then asks 'what one thing,' and Curly replies, 'That's for you to find out.'

"Well, what I think Curly was talking about was focusing on and finding one thing to do, and doing it well with all of your heart, soul and brain. I've thought about that a lot, even if I haven't lived it so well. But I do think there's value in focusing on one thing and I believe that Anorah has that one thing down to an art. What do you think?"

"I hadn't thought of that, John," offered Lori. "But you're right. She really focuses on one thing, and goes after it no matter what, and she usually gets what she wants. But I've also noticed," she continued, "that when she doesn't seem to have something to focus on, a toy to find, or a new corner to explore, a goal as it were, she just sits in the middle of the room and cries."

"You know, you're on to something there kiddo. That's just how I feel when I don't have a goal or focus," I chuckled.

Lori said, "Maybe Curly knew what he was talking about. After all, it does seem to work for Anorah. I wonder if it could work for us? Sometimes I feel so scattered that I never seem to get anything done. Maybe I should find one thing?"

"Me, too," I replied. "I guess, once again, I've learned something from my daughter, and, if I learn this lesson well, focus on one thing, do it well, and am not deterred by obstacles, then perhaps I'll find my toys, too!"

****

I am sometimes scattered in my efforts, and lack a purpose, or intent. During those times I am edgy, lack energy and seem to be unaccomplished. Viktor Frankl, the famed Austrian psychiatrist who survived the World War II German concentration camp, Treblinka, developed his powerful theory of Logotherapy, which is based upon the concept of seeking and then acting upon a personal purpose. That is, those who have a purpose, goals, and a focus are likely to be more successful, happier and more accomplished than those who lack goals and purpose. Focus, goals, a plan and single-minded determination are what allow Anorah to find her toys and have inspired me to do the same.

GUARDIAN ANGELS

We cannot pass our guardian angel's bounds, resigned or
sullen, he will hear our sighs.

~ John Keble ~

"Wow, I barely caught her." I rushed up the driveway of our
new house holding Anorah, who was oblivious to anything that
might be amiss, in my arms. My heart was pounding like a base
drum inside my chest, and my eyes must have been the size of
silver dollars.

"What happened?" Lori shot back, her deep concern regis-
tered in her voice and with her facial expression.

"Anorah and Alex (Alex is her toddler friend) were running
out to see Magic in the yard when she tripped over a rock on
the retaining wall and started falling face first over the wall and
onto the lower level of rocks. If she had fallen, she would've
really gotten hurt. She was lucky that I happened to be near her
and that I caught her," I reported. I was a bit shaken, which was
reflected in tenor of my words.

"It's a good thing you were there," Lori sighed. "That child
seems as though she's always this close to disaster," she commented with her fingers less than an inch apart. "It's a good
thing we're around whenever something dangerous occurs. And
the funny part is, she has no idea what almost happened to her."

"Yeah, I wish I had someone watching over me like that. It would be great to have a guardian angel or someone always keeping me away from disasters, wouldn't it? What's for dinner?" I asked, noticing that the fear in my belly had changed to pangs of hunger.

"I don't know. What are you making?" Lori kidded, knowing how much I dislike cooking.

"How about pizza?" I countered. "I can go to Little Caesar's and get a "pizza, pizza," their pizza is cheap and tastes pretty good," I offered as a way to get around my turn to cook.

"Okay, pizza it is," Lori agreed. "It's easier than cooking, and besides, we need to reward ourselves for all of the yard work we did today."

"Okay, I'll go order one. What do you want on it?"

"Get the big gooey supreme pizza; I'm really hungry," Lori implored.

I went into the house through the garage door, pushed aside a red garden rake that was lying on the garage floor, and thought to myself: "I've got to get some hooks put up so the rakes, shovels, and brooms are off the garage floor. Somebody could fall over them and get hurt." The near disaster with Anorah had heightened my safety concerns.

After I phoned in the pizza order, I washed up quickly, went back outside, and kissed Lori and Anorah goodbye.

"Be careful, John, the wind is picking up, and there's a severe thunderstorm warning." I just waved at her, thinking to myself how overly cautious she can be sometimes. Heading out in the Jeep, I decided to go through the neighborhood instead of the back way since it is more scenic.

I waved as I drove past our next-door neighbors who were outside doing some landscaping themselves. They seemed to be headed in. The neighborhood kids were everywhere, playing pitch and catch, street hockey, or chasing each other with their boundless energy. I imagined that their parents would call them in quickly, as I noticed that the wind was getting stronger, and the sky was turning a threatening black with huge dark thunderhead clouds. I honked the horn and waved to them, and continued on my way to town.

Driving slowly along Almena Drive into Kalamazoo, I was particularly careful to keep my speed below the 35 mile-per-hour limit. Anorah's near-accident had me on my toes. As I entered the intersection of Almena Drive and M-43 into Kalamazoo, I was mindful of how busy the traffic was and that I needed to be careful entering the main thoroughfare. A loud thud came from somewhere behind me and a gust of wind hit the Jeep causing it to sway slightly from side to side. I thought nothing of it and headed to Little Caesar's.

Upon picking up the pizza, I retraced the same route home. The smell of the pizza was making me ravenous with hunger, and I had to fight off the impulse to devour a piping hot wedge in the car. Lori is always teasing me about the partial pizzas that we seem to buy, so tonight I thought I'd surprise her and bring home a whole pizza. Besides, eating hot pizza while driving is not a smart thing to do. I grabbed a piece of hard candy from its tin and popped it into my mouth. "That should hold me until I get home," I thought to myself.

I pulled the Jeep into the garage, grabbed the still hot pizza box by the sides, and envisioned the first bite of pizza. My mouth was salivating in anticipation of cheese, pepperoni, onions, mushrooms, and green peppers draped over warm pizza dough. No sooner had I hit the door than Lori was animatedly gesturing to me: "John, I'm so glad you're home! Did you hear what happened? Are you all right?"

"Huh?" I replied dumbfounded, my thoughts of pizza replaced with fear and concern.

"What do you mean? What happened? Is Anorah all right?"

"Didn't you hear the sirens?"

"No. I didn't hear any sirens; I had the radio up and was listening to the Western football game (Western Michigan University was playing Central Michigan University). What are you talking about?"

"A tree fell in front of the Patterson's house."

"Wow. Is everybody okay? By Patterson's house, really?" I asked, even more concerned, since I had just seen Robb and Kathy Patterson outside raking leaves on this mid autumn day.

"What really alarmed me, John, is that I received a call from Kathy Patterson saying that it fell just as a Jeep exited the subdivision on to M-43. John, that tree just missed you."

My mind went blank for a second, and then I remembered the noise and the wind. "I thought I heard something as I was leaving and I knew it was really windy, but I never knew that I was in the path of a killer tree," I replied, making light of the situation while shaking a little inside.

"Well, I'm just glad that you're okay," Lori added as she gave me a big hug.

"I want a hug, too, Daddy. I want a hug, too," Anorah chimed in.

We gave hugs all around until I finally said: "How about some pizza?"

"Boy, John," Lori remarked half way through the pizza, "I wonder how close that tree really came to hitting you?"

"I don't know, Lori. The funny thing is, I was totally unaware of how close to disaster I really was. I'm always thinking how often Anorah is close to disaster and one of us will save her at the last possible second and how she is always unaware of what almost happened to her, and now I have a near disaster, too. Maybe just as we so closely watch over Anorah and keep her safe from harm, God or one of his Guardian Angels is doing the same for us. Maybe we, too, without the watchful eyes of God, would be much closer to disaster. That's something to think about it, isn't it?"

****

Joseph Girzone believes that *"your heavenly Father sends his Angels to watch over the little ones."* I suspect that within his plan He is watching over all of us. Many of us live our lives with little sense of what is going on in our immediate environment and even less of what may be happening all around us. My incident with Anorah and then my near miss with the tree in the storm caused me to think about how I always have one eye peeled on Anorah. Most parents are like that. More times than I can count I have "rescued" Anorah from one kind of a near disaster or another. Whether she is nearly tumbling off a retaining wall, trying to eat something that she shouldn't eat, drinking out of the birdbath, grabbing a pair of misplaced scissors, or nearly anything else, her daddy or her momma has saved her from disasters, ones that for the most part are unknown to Anorah both in their occurrence and their potential consequences. Maybe just as she is oblivious to her near disasters, we, too, are being protected from our near disasters by a higher power.

JUST LIKE A CHILD

I see everything as a little child would and have never lost my sense of wonder. It is as fresh today as it was at the very beginning. I look across creation each day and see that it is good. The balance in creation is vivid evidence of God's genius.

—*Joseph Girzone*

"I'm not sure that I can do this, John. What if I hit another boat or run over a skier? What if I ruin the motor or something? I've never done this before, you know," Lori pleaded uncertainly.

The surface of Sherman Lake was nearly calm, yet I could feel the cool spray of the water on my face on that 90-degree Michigan summer afternoon. I had just taken Lori water skiing and offered to let her take a turn at piloting the boat across the lake. Earlier in the day, she had shown interest in trying her hand on this small inland lake, but now she was nervous and unsure if she really wanted to pilot the boat after all. It's not a big boat, only about 19 feet or so, and the lake was placid and mostly unused at this time so it was an excellent time for her first turn at the helm.

"Oh, John, maybe I shouldn't. Maybe I should just let you drive the boat; okay?

"Sure, Lori," I replied rather amused by her sudden change of face, "but it's no different than driving a car, except the traffic flow is not as predictable so you just have to pay attention more closely."

"I'll drive, Daddy. Let me drive the boat. I can do it, can't I, Daddy?" Anorah suddenly offered with equal parts of youthful enthusiasm and naivete.

"Oh, Anorah," I responded. "I'd love to let you drive the boat, but you're not old enough, honey. But I am proud of you for asking and wanting to try."

"Please, Daddy, I can do it. I'm not afraid, really Daddy, please."

"In a few years when you're older, honey, then you can drive the boat; okay?"

"Oh, Daddy, you always say that. You always say when I'm older. When will I be old enough, Daddy?"

"Soon enough, Anorah. I don't want you to grow up too fast, honey. I like you just the way you are for now," I said while piloting the boat.

Anorah seemed to have accepted her plight and was watching the water crest over the bow as it sped along. "Daddy, Daddy, go faster Okay? The water is getting my face all wet and I like that, so go faster!" Anorah had quickly gotten over her desire to pilot that boat, and for that I was happy.

"Okay, John, I'll drive the boat," Lori announced unexpectedly. "If Anorah has the courage to ask to drive the boat, then I need to model that for her and have the courage myself, now don't I?"

"Yep, you may as well go for it," I agreed. Lori slid beneath the steering wheel and clutched it somewhat tentatively.

"What do I do now, John?" she asked wide-eyed and with a tiny quiver in her voice.

"First, we need to put another cushion on top of your seat so you can see over the wheel." For some reason the seats in these small powerboats are somewhat low and anybody piloting this boat would have a hard time seeing over the steering wheel, especially when it is at full throttle and the bow raises up high. I am 6'4" and it is even difficult for me to see over the wheel easily, so Lori's diminutive height of 5'4" really puts her at a disadvantage. I put a blue and red cushion beneath her. I added another one for even more height. "Now this is the throttle and pushing it forward makes the boat go forward, and on the throttle is a trim switch..."

The lesson went on until Lori decided that she had grasped my instructions. She pushed the throttle forward, adjusted speed, and steered as if she had been piloting boats her whole life. After an hour or so, we decided to head back to the dock. Anorah was tired, bored, and getting a bit cranky. We were all hungry and thirsty, a little tired, and a beautiful crimson and gold sunset was vividly emerging onto the horizon, signaling that it was time to head for shore.

Upon pulling up to the dock, I jumped out and tied a line to the dock before jogging over to the Jeep. I always dislike putting the boat back onto the trailer, as it seems to have a mind of its own. However, this time I successfully bulldogged it onto the trailer on the first try! More often than not, I load the boat onto the trailer a bit cockeyed and then I have to back the trailer into the water, get out of the Jeep, walk back into the water myself and start the process all over again. So I was delighted to have gotten it on right the first time.

The ride home found us surrounded by darkness as the earlier sunset seems to have disappeared much too quickly. Anorah fell into a peaceful sleep in the back of the Jeep in her child safety seat. Lori and I drove silently into the night, listening to the crickets and bullfrogs engage in their nightly discourse.

Lori was first to break the silence. "I'm really glad that I drove the boat today, John. It was a lot more fun than I thought it was going to be, and you know what, I wouldn't have done it if it weren't for Anorah. She inspired and embarrassed me all at the same time. Here she is, three years old and more than willing to drive the boat, not a fear in the world, and I'm in my thirties and timid as a bunny rabbit. It's funny, too, because I was thinking about the sermon in church last week and how the minister was talking about how Jesus wants us to be like a child."

Although I was getting dog tired from the long day and all of the driving and bulldogging the boat, I was trying to listen attentively. Lori's conversation and my trying to pull the Jeep into the driveway without running over the newly planted rhododendron lining the side of the driveway had split my concentration.

"Huh? Hold on a second. I'm sorry, honey," I apologized for breaking her train of thought, "I'm listening now."

Lori continued, "What's even more interesting to me is how the minister presented her interpretation of what Jesus meant by being like a child. Remember how she talked about how children are honest, trusting, forgiving, hopeful, innocent, and loving? All of that is true, but after Anorah's adventurous behavior today, I think that there are other very important characteristics of children that Jesus would like us to emulate. Children are also adventuresome, curious, and willing to take risks to learn and experience new things. It seems that so many of us as adults have lost that childlike sense of wonderment and adventure we once had."

"We are no longer like a child, but become risk aversive as adults and get into a comfortable, but unrewarding, complacent rut," I added to show her that I was in tune with her thoughts.

"And," Lori continued, "you know what Earl Nightingale said about ruts, don't you?"

"No. What did old Earl say about ruts?"

"John! You're the one who told me. He said, 'A rut is nothing more than a grave with the ends kicked out.' Maybe that's what Jesus meant, too?"

I reflected upon Lori's interpretation of our adventure today as I left the Jeep.

I unhooked the boat trailer and pulled the Jeep into the garage where our dog Magic was eagerly waiting to greet us and I suspect to visit with his buddy, the sleeping Anorah.

I turned to Lori and said: "You've offered a really unique interpretation. Looking at it from your perspective, maybe I should be more like a child and refine my child like curiosity, sense of adventure, and fearlessness. Like a child, huh, what a great way to live."

****

We are frequently so full of the fear of failure that we often don't take risks, don't explore our potential, sometimes lose our sense of wonderment, drop our goals, and end up living in that rut that Earl Nightingale described. More often than not, I hear a million reasons from friends and co-workers about why something can't be done instead of the focus on why it can be done. While visiting with my in-laws, Richard and Dorothy Perkins, in Oregon, I found a small embroidered and framed proverb in a small tourist shop:

> "Whether you believe you can do something, or you believe you can't, you're right."

I hung that idiom in my office and refer to it daily, especially in times of doubt. Former U.S. Attorney General and assassinated presidential candidate Robert Kennedy is reported to have said, "There are those who look at things the way they are, and ask why? I dream of things that never were, and ask why not?" (Kennedy may have borrowed this from George Bernard Shaw). Kennedy, the great leader, also said *"Only those who dare to fail greatly can ever achieve greatly,"* was speaking as a child in seeing the possibilities of life without the fear of failure, and the doubts that nag so many of us. I am on the way to my own personal journey of adventure, possibilities and seeing what can be, and not what can't be. And while each and every step is fraught with fear, and uncertainty about the unseen outcomes, I am certain that this is the journey that I must take; and those fears are the ones that I must face, just like a child. In this spirit, I cite Ralph Waldo Emerson, who advised to *"Always do what you are afraid to do."*

BE HERE NOW!

If you surrender completely to the moments as they pass,
you live more richly those moments.

~ Anne Morrow Lindbergh ~

"Did you bring me a surprise, Daddy?" were the first words I heard from Anorah as I entered the house. I was loaded down with my pastel suitcase, the one with the broken wheels. The suitcase was lumpy from my habit of simply throwing mounds of clothes into it after a trip without folding anything. It held an assortment of odd-shaped gifts and souvenirs and seemed to weigh a ton. I also had a bag from the San Francisco-based candy store Ghiradelli, and an old brown leather briefcase. Somewhere in that mess was a present for Anorah.

"Yes, honey, of course I brought you a present. I gave her a broad smile as I knelt down and reached toward her. "But how about if you give your daddy a big hug and a kiss first?"

"Okay, Daddy," Anorah agreed as she jumped into my arms and began giving me hugs and kisses. Then she quickly broke free and asked: "Can I have my present now?"

"You sure can, but first let me say hello to your mommy." I gave Lori a kiss. I rummaged through my suitcase and handed Anorah a Native American Barbie doll that I had purchased at a quaint little shop that specialized in such things. Anorah squealed with delight. Her bright eyes danced all over the doll. Then she hugged it close to her chest and swayed from side to side in the loving manner Lori uses to soothe her when she is upset.

"Oh, Daddy, it's just what I wanted. Thank you. I'm really happy! What should I call her, Daddy?" Anorah asked one second and then interjected immediately before I could answer: "I know, I'll call her Pocahontas. That's what I'll call her. What do you think, Daddy?"

"I think that's great name, honey. Pocahontas is a great name." Anorah had just seen the Disney video *Pocahontas*.

I had just returned from a four-day business trip to San Francisco, which had included most of the weekend, and I was grateful to be home. In a few days we would be off on a family trip to Mackinac Island in northern Michigan, so I was going to savor every minute home until then. After a few minutes visiting with Lori, I knew that I was back to the reality of daily life.

So I dragged my suitcase behind me and headed off to the bedroom to unpack it. It was already near bedtime with the west to east time change, so I knew that we should not be up much later; but I was still revved up from my trip and sleep would not come easily for the others or me. Because of the excitement of my return, we stayed up a little later. It was summer after all. The evening settled down, and Anorah was busy playing with Pocahontas, while I shared the excitement and the highlights of my trip with Lori.

"I have to admit that San Francisco is one beautiful city," I gushed. "It's everything they say that it is. And that's coming from a diehard, loyal, no holds barred Cleveland boy," I added for emphasis.

"What was the high point of your trip?" Lori beamed as she readjusted her position on the couch to face me. Lori was fond of telling people that she was a "fourth—generation Californian," so my gushing about San Francisco was like Christmas in July for her.

"Oh, there were so many. The view from Golden Gate Bridge was incredible. It was sunny that day and nearly blinding, but it only enhanced the gently waving blue waters and the real sense of enchantment that I felt. I was even more delighted when our bus driver told us that the sunshine over the bridge and bay is somewhat rare because fog usually shrouds the view, so I felt especially lucky. Near the bridge was really quite an experience. There were vendors everywhere, mostly selling clothes and jewelry. I was amazed with the range of wares that were for sale, but even more amazed when on a couple of occasions they packed up and were gone nearly instantaneously. Someone me told me that they did not have permits, and that the police were lurking nearby."

"My most memorable experience, though, was the boat ride I took on Oakland Bay. Just being on the water and watching the other boats glide by was so tranquil. Looking at all of the magnificent homes that line the shore was awesome. There are some very wealthy people in the Bay area judging from the size of those houses!" And feeling the warm breeze with an occasional wisp of mist on my face when the wind and waves picked up was heavenly. I was relaxed, with nowhere to go, nothing to do, and not a worry in the world. I was really living in the moment and thoroughly enjoying where I was."

"Did you see a big whale, Daddy?" Anorah suddenly broke in to our conversation. I wasn't aware that she was listening, but then I've read somewhere that toddlers are like little anthropologists, always scoping out the scene and observing even when you think they aren't listening or observing.

"No, Anorah, I didn't see any whales. I don't think they have whales in that bay." I tried to explain, but not knowing much about the migratory patterns of whales limited my description. I was sure, though, that I hadn't seen any that day.

"Actually, John, there are whales in the bay, I think" commented my wife, the fourth generation Californian, with a hesitant laugh.

"Oh, okay, Daddy. Well, did you have fun on your boat ride in the ocean?" She continued to quiz me while adjusting Pocahontas's torso into a sitting position and combing her hair with a mini doll comb.

"I had a great time, honey. It was almost perfect except that you and Mommy weren't there. Then it would have been perfect."

"Okay, Daddy, well when I'm old enough to go on vacation, I want to go on a boat ride with you and Mommy. Okay, Daddy? Can we take Pocahontas with us?"

"You bet, honey. We will all go on a boat ride soon next week on our vacation when we take the ferry to Mackinac Island, and we'll take Pocahontas along with us, too."

"What's a ferry, Daddy?"

"It's another name for a boat," Lori added.

The next week went by quickly. I returned to work and since Lori has summers off as a teacher, she and Anorah went to music lessons and horse camp. Anorah has always loved horses, and this was her first summer of riding. Her horse is a spotted white Appaloosa named Cody. Cody is very gentle, which is a good thing for a little girl not yet four. Before I knew it, our vacation beckoned. We arose early that morning, which is unusual for us, and we were in the Jeep and on the road before the crack of dawn. After an easy six-hour drive on a cloudless day with only three potty breaks, one of which we combined with a short trip to McDonalds, we found ourselves on a ferry-boat headed to Mackinac Island, which is located in the straits in Lake Huron near Michigan's Upper Peninsula.

That mid-August day was vibrantly sunny, although a brisk breeze whipped across the straits and into our faces, chilling us slightly. The ferry was rocking gently in the waves, and water sprayed all around us. Anorah clung tightly to me, and Lori had her arms wrapped around both us. I felt connected to them in a way that I had never thought possible.

"Boy, I can't wait to get over to the island. I really want to show it to you. It's been a long time since I've been there. I sure wish that this boat ride was over," I commented as we looked out into the distance with more than a slight feeling of impatience. "Are you having fun, Anorah?" I asked, suddenly aware that she was clinging to me rather tightly.

"Yes, Daddy, I think it's great!" she exclaimed with a huge smile, her soft hazel eyes looking up at me.

"She really is enjoying the moment, I thought to myself." "Well, just wait until we get to Mackinac Island. Then you'll really have a good time!" I was hoping to transmit my excitement about the island to her. "Not only is the governor's mansion there, but a very special movie called *Somewhere in Time* was filmed at the Grand Hotel."

"What's the governor, Daddy?" she asked.

"He's the boss of Michigan," I replied.

"Oh, Daddy, I thought Momma was the boss," Anorah added. Just then a big wave caused the boat to roll a bit and Anorah clung even tighter.

"WOW! That was fun; I'm really having a good time now, Daddy. Besides, you told me that when you took a boat trip with Mommy and me, it would be perfect, didn't you, Daddy? Yes or no?" she added, as if to pin me down.

She hardly forgets anything. Once again she had reminded me of something I thought was inconsequential but was important to her. "Yes, Anorah, you're right; it is perfect with you and Mommy. I'm so glad to be here. Thanks for reminding me." "Anorah is right. There is no place I would rather be than with my family enjoying this moment," I thought to myself.

A sudden gust of cool air refocused my thoughts back to the moment. The deep blue water color in the Straits was almost astonishing, and I had to squint to keep from being blinded by the combination of sunlight and its reflection off the water. A lone seagull dive-bombed near the boat. "Maybe," I thought, "he is used to getting scraps of food from the tourists, or maybe he's just a free spirit in search of adventure?" I may have missed him or other aspects of our trip to Mackinac Island had Anorah not reminded me of what I said only a few days earlier. "Oh Daddy, this is so much fun on the boat ride with you and Momma. Thank you!"

****

My mind is too often somewhere else and not enjoying the moment. My most difficult lesson is to live in and enjoy the here and now. No matter where I am or what I am doing, I strive to enjoy that moment for all it is worth. In San Francisco, the bay tour was the main event, and I accepted it as such. Yet it was a boat ride, no more, and no less than the one across the Michigan Straits. When we took the ferry across the Straits of Mackinac, I was looking forward to the future, getting to the island, and not enjoying the moment. As I reflected upon it, I realized that each event, each boat ride was basically the same, but how I perceived each one was different. I concluded that the present is real, and it's now.

Plus, in order to be healthy and whole following my difficult childhood, I've had to learn to live in the present and not in the past. I've met so many people who are trapped by their history and are seemingly unable to overcome whatever transgressions have come their way. Stephen Covey advises us to live out our imaginations and not our history.

As I reflected upon both of my boat trips, I realized that each in its own moment had its place. To be not mentally in the present was to miss a part of my life as it was happening. I can do nothing about the past, and the future is still an illusion. Now I am learning to live in the present. After all, the rest is either history or fantasy, by living in the past, or by living in the future, I was not living in the present. My mind was elsewhere and I was missing out on the wondrous present, the only moment that I have. After all, life is a series of moments, and each moment is a blessing and a choice. When we are not in the moment and are someplace else, we deny ourselves the present moment, the only one that we really have. Someone once said that it is called the present because it is a gift.

But You Like to Play with Me

Always think in terms of what the other person wants.
~ James Van Fleet ~

"Daddy, will you play in the pool with me? Daddy?" Anorah was pleading from the green plastic wading pool shaped like a turtle. Lori and I had spent most of the afternoon raking, weeding, and planting flower beds. This was the first summer in our new home and, like many of our neighbors, we were taking advantage of the warm weekend to spruce up the exterior.

"No, honey, I don't want to play in the pool with you right now. I have a lot more work to do, and I really don't want to get wet," I explained, thrusting a handful of weeds, one which pricked my finger, and drawing a small droplet of blood, deep into a large black Hefty brand trash bag.

"Oh please, Daddy, please play with me in the pool! We'll have so much fun," Anorah begged, her lower lip pushed out to emphasize her displeasure with me.

"No, not now, honey. I don't want to get wet. I have to do some more work." I was a little perturbed by her persistence but trying not to show it. "Can't she see that I'm busy?" I wondered to myself.

"But you like to play with me, Daddy," Anorah reminded me. I know that I give in to her whims easily, but I love her so much and there was never anyone there to pamper me when I was her age. "I don't ever want to fail her like my parents failed me, I thought to myself."

"Alright, honey, let me put on my swim-suit, and I'll get into the pool with you. Will that make you happy?"

"Yes. Hurry, Daddy, okay?" Anorah squealed triumphantly. I dropped the rake onto the weed-filled trash bag, patted Anorah on the head, and exited the back yard. The rear door was still locked from our trip to the hardware store so I went into the house through the garage, where the dog lay on a brown and white rectangular mat panting from the heat.

"Hey Magic! I chortled, "I guess you're about to get a bath." He seemed unimpressed. I scurried up the stairway and into the bedroom, walked past the unmade, cherry, four poster bed, through the bathroom, and into the closet. I quickly spotted my swimming trunks.

I was in the pool only about 15 minutes when I got out and coaxed Anorah out, too, since she had been in the water about a half-hour. I didn't want her to get sick, since she was only about a week removed from a cold. Lori came over from washing the dog and dried Anorah off. "What, you're not going to dry me off, too?" I ask buoyantly. Lori merely chuckled and took Anorah into the house to get dressed.

"Can I watch Wishbone, Daddy?" (Wishbone is her favorite video about a dog that assumes the role of hero in various settings.) "And I want some hot chocolate, too."

"Sure honey, you can watch Wishbone and maybe Momma will fix you some hot chocolate," I replied. Sure enough, almost before I have settled in, Lori has brought hot chocolate for

Anorah and a diet Coke for me. For some reason, Anorah likes hot chocolate in the summer, too. I guess she was just chilled from the pool. Together we watched Wishbone and his high jinks, when soon we saw that Anorah had fallen asleep watching TV.

"John, Lori whispered so not to wake Anorah, why did you get into that cold pool with her? I was impressed."

"She made a really persuasive and compelling point, which convinced me that I wanted to be in the pool with her despite the cold water, even though I didn't want to get undressed and I had work to do."

"What point was that?" Lori asked.

"Well, she said something like, 'But you like to play with me.' I thought that was so profound, and it appealed to my self-interest in addition to her own; there was no way that I could refuse."

"What do you mean?" Lori asked.

"Think about how intuitively clever her approach was. She didn't say, 'Daddy, I want you in the pool with me' or something else that focused only on her interests and needs. Instead she appealed to my self-interest and why it was a good idea for me to get into the pool. I was so struck by her approach that getting into the pool was the only real option. And, just as importantly, she was right. I do like to play with her. So not only did she appeal to my self-interest, she did it accurately. I'm going to think about this for a long time and try to be more mindful of understanding what someone else wants and needs and try to put that first over what I might want and need."

"You know, John, I have to admit, you do have an ability to pick those everyday experiences out of the air and turn them into meaningful lessons. It kind of reminds me of Stephen Covey's 4th habit, Seek first to understand, then to be understood."

"Maybe Anorah's been reading Covey," I laughed as we headed back to the lawn work while Anorah napped.

****

Most of us have goals, agendas, and things that we want. But we are sometimes unmindful that others also have goals, agendas and things that they want. As a result we often focus solely on our own needs, our own wants and our own desires, sometimes to the exclusion of what others want, need or desire. Earl Nightingale wisely noted that everything that we have, we must get with and through people. It is in our best interest to be generous, thoughtful, and to put other's needs and wants almost on a par with our own, if not above. In that way, by serving others, we are more likely to get our own needs and wants met; Anorah did when she compelled me with her "but you like to play with me" statement, and in the end we were both happier.

THE DETOUR

There are those who travel and those who are going some-
where. They are different and yet they are the same. The
success has this over his rivals: He knows where he is going.
~ Mark Caine ~

Pulling out of the parking lot, I am mindful of my directions, the increasing darkness, the unfamiliar rental car, and my need to get to the Hartford airport on time in order to catch my flight home. I had recently been laid off from my job with a local mental health agency in Kalamazoo and had flown to Hartford, Connecticut, to interview for a job as a program evaluator with an agency that serves at-risk youth. I am a native Midwesterner and have only been on the East Coast a few times; in spite of my eagerness to return home, the history, beauty, and grandeur of the New England area almost stun me.

Driving at a moderate speed following the interview, I carefully watch the road signs until I find the entrance to the interstate and breathe a sigh of relief. I am happy to be on the highway and know that it will quickly take me to the airport to catch my plane. The traffic is thick and fast. Visibility is limited by the increasing darkness and the heavy swirling snows. I don't know the Hartford area, since I've never been here, so I drive very cautiously.

73

I constantly find myself being passed by most cars and note that others are tailgating. I am uncomfortable and a little bit anxious. Driving along Interstate 84 East, I am mindful to locate the off ramp to highway 91 north and the service road to Bradley Field Airport Road, which is exit 40. As I near the Bradley Field Airport Road exit, I slow down, being careful to avoid slip sliding away in the icy road conditions. I squint into very bright highway lights, the lights of on-coming traffic, and a slight snow squall. I am a little disoriented. I finally see my exit and get off. I'm glad that this part of my journey is almost over and relieved to be that much closer to the airport and to my family.

I immediately feel a jolt of panic as I realize that I have left the interstate one exit early and gotten off instead at the Kennedy Road exit. "Yikes, I quickly tell myself, I really messed up." Then I realize that I can simply and easily return to the highway on the overpass ramp and find the correct exit. To my consternation, I find that I cannot get back on the highway quite that easily. There is a detour and in order to get back on the highway, I have to follow the detour. "Great. Not only am I in a strange city at night in the winter in a rental car, but I'm now on a detour, of all things," I tell myself.

Momentarily annoyed, I have visions of getting lost, perhaps in a dangerous area, or missing my plane and getting stranded in Hartford for the night. I don't want to miss seeing Lori and Anorah today . My windshield wipers are barely adequate for the task of removing the increasingly heavy snows, and I am now on a two-lane road winding through the city, a city that seems dark, foreboding and impersonal. I wonder why this detour must be through such a dark, desolate part of the city. I am somewhat afraid that I will miss my flight. The thought of spending the night in Hartford is not at all appealing. I keep my doors locked and continue to focus on the detour signs, but I am increasingly aware of the time.

Soon, the detour takes me into what seems to be a more rural area. I follow the detour signs and curse my luck at missing my exit. Then I notice that in the darkness the countryside is beautiful. The moon has emerged through an opening in the clouds. The snowflakes, falling lighter now, paint a Currier and Ives Christmas scene. I am less fretful and even am starting to enjoy the moment. Twinkling and nearly mesmerizing Christmas lights outline homes along the road, and I start to feel a sense of wonderment at the Season and am almost happy to have gotten lost.

I realize that if I had not missed my original exit, I would not have experienced the beautiful Connecticut countryside. I relax somewhat and realize that I will get to the airport; I've just taken a different route than I expected. The detour takes me where it is supposed to, to the airport. I arrive in plenty of time, safe and unscathed. I turn in my rental car, a gold Dodge Neon, at the Hertz desk, hand the gate attendant my boarding pass, and enter the aircraft. I sit in my seat, delighted and a little surprised to be on the way home to family. Yup, I board the plane one happy guy and gladly take the complimentary diet Coke offered by the attendant and settle in to read the *USA Today* newspaper.

Reading the newspaper doesn't come easily though, and I sit on the plane and reflect upon my circuitous route to my destination. I realize that rather than being lost, I was on a journey that enriched me, which I would not have had unless I had taken a wrong turn and gone on the detour. It occurs to me that life is often a series of detours taken on the way to our destination, wherever it is. We often are sent toward our destiny along a different route than we had planned. We fight that detour sometimes, bemoan our bad luck and curse the obstacles that we think the fates have thrown our way.

Yet, we can still keep our eyes on our goal and at the same time enjoy the new unexpected sights, sounds and new relationships that we are now experiencing. Our lives are enriched in ways that we had not expected, and perhaps we even have new goals, maybe even better goals that will take us to higher highs. After all, we've had new experiences and our horizons have expanded.

I am reminded of the good luck, bad luck story. A farmer's only plow horse has run off into the mountains. The sturdy horse did much of the work around the small farm and, upon learning of the loss, the neighbors, a friendly and caring lot, came to console the farmer. The farmer, a taciturn and laconic man, simply responded to his neighbors' concern with "Good luck, bad luck, who knows?"

The neighbors walked away scratching their heads and wondering about the farmer's tranquil attitude. "What does he mean?" they asked one another. "It seems like only bad luck to us." A few days later, the farmer's horse returned from the mountains, in the company of several other new horses, all of which were wild mustangs. The word soon spread throughout the small, close-knit community. All of the neighbors descended upon the farmer to congratulate him upon his good fortune.

However, they were surprised to find that the farmer was no more excited about having his original horse return than in having two additional horses to work around the farm. He was no more concerned than when his original horse disappeared. Once again, the farmer simply said "Good luck, bad luck, who knows?" Puzzled, the neighbors left, wondering about their strange neighbor. They kept close note of the farmer and his son as they trained the new horses. Thus, they were keenly aware when the son broke his leg while being kicked during training.

Thinking that surely the farmer would be devastated by having his only son's leg broken, they were less than surprised when, after offering their condolences, the farmer simply responded, "Good luck, bad luck, who knows?" At this point, the neighbors were convinced that their friend had a screw loose, that is until a war broke out with a neighboring country shortly thereafter, and the son, due to his broken leg, was not able to go to war. Good luck, bad luck, indeed; who does know?

****

I reflect upon my Hartford detour often as I go on my journeys and am sometimes sidetracked, either on an actual trip, or from a cherished goal. Sometimes I am momentarily confused about why my chosen path was taken from me and, frustrated and angry that something did not work out as I planned and expected. When I reflect upon the Hartford detour, I regain confidence that my detour may not be bad luck, and what I may find, in spite of my fears, may still be good luck. It's nearly impossible for us to know what God has in store for us, or where his plan may take us. Yet, even though doors are closing, new mountain peaks to scale suddenly appear where there was once a valley, and formerly open roads are unexpectedly closed to us, we are still on a journey. Perhaps, like my journey on the way home to my family from Hartford, our momentary detour and new path is really a road map laid out by God that is even more spectacular and enriching than any we had imagined.

EPILOGUE:
A JOURNEY WELL WORTH HAVING

Knock, knock, knock. Knock, knock, knock. The noise in my head would not cease. I ignored it, told it I was busy, I told it I was not at home, I told it I had too many other important things to do. I told it that I had a life to live! After all, I have a daughter to raise and did not have time to listen to inner voices, or messages from God. Finally, I gave in, and knew that the knocking had to be answered. *God Is In The Kitchen* would not let me rest, would not give me peace, and would not let me lie about my whereabouts, or make excuses until I had told its story.

It's been on my mind for nearly five years, five years of guilt for procrastinating so long, five years of near fear for thoughts that it might not get published; and, more importantly, five years of joy, awe, appreciation and excitement for the gifts that God has given me through Anorah. Finally, fear faded, and *God Is In The Kitchen* is real.

There is a wisdom claimed from my journey, both as a reluctant father, and as a survivor of child abuse, child neglect, and from having moved at least 60 different times from my childhood to my young adulthood. I am grateful for having had this journey, which has given me an insight that cannot be taught in school, university, or from a study. But still it may be shared in the hope that my experiences can be shared. I have had, and am on, a delightful journey, which has formed the mosaic of many lessons.

Several years ago, Michigan Governor John Engler invited me to serve on a statewide commission called the "Children's Commission." The purpose of this commission was to examine and evaluate practices, policies, and laws related to child welfare in the state of Michigan. Up to that point in my life I had had very little contact with powerful, highly visible and successful people, so my confidence was in a bit of short supply, and this commission was filled with visible and successful people.

Still I was honored to be selected and very much looked forward to participating. I drove up to Lansing, Michigan, the state capitol, with great anticipation. After getting lost in the very large and magnificent capitol building, I finally got a set of directions to the meeting room from a suspicious, uniformed security guard unsure of my business.

The room was appointed with a very ornate, long, heavy, and highly glossed cherry table. Around the table were matching cherry chairs with virgin white upholstered pads that looked as though they had been directly imported in a time warp from the Elizabethan Period. Further adding to the grandeur of the setting were wide black and white marble windowsills and long hanging royal purple curtains hung with gold-colored curtain rods adorning windows that seemed to be at least 15 feet tall. Needless to say, I was awestruck. Most of the state cabinet-level members as well as selected state luminaries were in attendance. Also in attendance was John Seita, me. I did not think I belonged. No wonder the security guard was suspicious. I was somewhat scared. Then over time a miracle happened, one that I never could have imagined from my days as a small, frail and abused child.

After several meetings in the State Capitol in these regal settings with this august body, I returned home and commented to Lori that I had good news and bad news. "What's the good news, John?"

"Well, I replied somewhat cautiously and with trepidation we're just as smart as the people leading the state of Michigan."

"What's the bad news, then?" she asked almost as cautiously. "We're just as smart as the people leading the state of Michigan."

"Really!" she replied with a measure of barely concealed doubt. "Why?"

"Well, this committee is very dedicated, very caring, and we have the best interests of Michigan's children at heart. However, in many ways, they are just as confused and unsure as we are about child welfare and things in general as the rest of us. And all of the trappings are simply trappings just like the great Oz in the movie *Wizard of Oz*. And as I thought about it, Lori, this discovery is both a blessing and a curse. It is a blessing since I know now that I should not look to others to be more capable, more able, or more willing to make a difference than either you or me.

On the other hand, this new knowledge now suggests to me that we have no excuses for not making a difference, taking charge of our own lives and for not grabbing life by the horns. We have new responsibilities, based upon this knowledge and have the power within us to choose to use that responsibility to make a difference."

I don't know where the next miracle is going to come from, what lessons I may learn from Anorah, Lori, or even you, but I do know that more will occur and that I will learn. I invite all of you to share your miracles with me, and I in turn will pass them along, so that together we can celebrate all of our miracles, all of our divinity, and be collectively and individually comforted and at peace knowing that *God Is In The Kitchen.*

ABOUT THE AUTHOR

Dr. John R. Seita is the President of the *Evaluation and Advocacy Group* in Kalamazoo, Michigan. He is a strong and forceful advocate of children and children's rights, especially children who are abused and neglected. His own autobiography, *In Whose_Best Interest,* chronicles his own experiences as an abused and neglected child. He is a frequent keynote speaker on the topic of children's rights and provides training and technical assistance on working with youth. He also provides nonprofit management and program evaluation consulting to agencies that serve children. He serves as an advisor to policymaking bodies on youth issues and on several nonprofit boards.

Dr. Seita is also affiliated with Reclaiming Youth International. He holds bachelor's master's, and doctoral degrees from Western Michigan University. He has been married to Lori for 12 years and, of course, Anorah is five. Dr. Seita may be contacted toll free at 1-888-647-2532 for keynote speeches on motivational topics, youth development, or program evaluation.

REFERENCES

Bach, R. (1989). *One*. New York: Dell.

Chapin, H. (1988). *Gold Metal Collection* (Compact Disk). : WEA/Electra:

Chopra, D. (2000). *How to Know God: The Soul's Journey Into the Mystery of Mysteries*: New York. Harmony Books.

Coelho, P. (1993). *The Alchemist: A Fable about Following Your Dreams*: San Francisco: Harper.

Covey, S. (1990). *The 7 Habits of Highly Effective People: Powerful Lessons in Personal Change*. New York: Simon and Schuster.

Dickens, C. (1981). *The Works of Charles Dickens: Complete and Unabridged*. London, England: Octopus Books, Limited.

Dyer, W. (1992). *Real Magic*. New York: Harper Paperbacks.

Dyer, W. (1989). *You'll See It When You Believe It: The Way to Personal Transformation*: New York: Avon Books.

Emerson, R. W. (Internet citation). http://www.privorich.com/quotes

Frankel, F. (1984). *Once Upon a Potty*. Hauppauge: Barron's Educational Services, Inc.

Frankel, V. (2000). *Man's Search for Meaning*. Beacon Press: Boston.

Grisham, J. (1995). *The Rainmaker*. New York. Doubleday Books.

Girzone, J. (2000). *Joshua The Homecoming*. Thornkike: Me.G.K. Hall and Company.

Hemingway, E. (1997). *A Farewell to Arms*. New York: Scribner:

Kennedy, R. (Internet citation) http://www.famous_quotations. Com.

McCant, J. cited in Cook, J.(Ed). (1999). The Book of Positive Quotations. Grammercy:

Nightingale, E. (1989). *The New Lead The Field*. (Audiotape). Chicago: Nightingale-Contant.

Poe, E.A. (1983). *18 Best Stories by Edgar Allan Poe*. New York: Dell.

Seita, J., Mitchell, M. & Tobin, C. (1996). *In Whose Best Interest? One Child's Odyssey, A Nation's Responsibility*: Elizabethtown. Pennsylvania, Continental Press.

Twain, M. Cited Cook, J. (1999). *The Book of Positive Quotations*. Grammercy:

Pittman, K. & Irby, M. (1996). Preventing problems or promoting development: Competing priorities or inseparable goals? International Youth Foundation. (Internet article) http://www.iyfnet.org/programs/preventingprob.html.

Printed in the United States
48303LVS00003B/153